PRESS FOR CHAMPAGNE

PRESS FOR CHAMPAGNE

A GUIDE TO ENJOYING THE WORLD'S GREATEST SPARKLING WINE

CHRISTOPHER S. RUHLAND

To Amy, who has given me love and support

and

Perry and Emmett, who have given me purpose

Contents

Press for Champagne

Wᴜᴀᴛ ɪꜰ ᴅᴇʟɪᴠᴇʀɪɴɢ ʙʟɪss ᴛᴏ sᴏᴍᴇᴏɴᴇ were as simple as connecting a button to a wire? I imagine that's the question the proprietor of Bob Bob Ricard, an eclectic yet elegant London diner, must have asked when configuring the restaurant. Because, while the restaurant features many unusual and amusing design elements and menu items, nobody on the other side of the world ever would have heard of the place if it weren't for a single stroke of genius. Bob Bob Ricard installed buttons at each booth marked "Press for Champagne." Press the button from your booth, and a waiter appears to hand you a glass of Champagne. Just think for a moment about sliding into one of those booths and noticing the button. How tempted are you to press it? Do you smile just thinking about it? Yeah. I do too.

This is the magic of Champagne. You only have to speak of it to make somebody happy. Plenty of wines are wonderful and delicious, but no wine delivers more immediate joy, laughter, surprise, and conviviality among wine drinkers than Champagne. There is a sense in which Champagne seems like it belongs not in the category of wine but in a special bucket of life's pleasures that predictably cause us to rejoice. And it delivers on its promise virtually every time. This is why we love Champagne.

Like anything magical, though, Champagne is mysteriously enchanting in a way that feels supernatural, inexplicable. What's going on in the glass of Champagne in your hand that makes it taste different from another Champagne? Why do you like one Champagne more than another, and, perhaps more importantly, how can you identify other Champagnes that are similar to the ones you enjoy the most? Are there other types and styles of Champagne that you haven't tried but would love if you did? And how would you even go about finding the answers to these questions? These are the questions asked by the curious Champagne drinker, the person who enjoys Champagne but who correctly intuits that there is so much more joy to be unlocked.

As someone who has spent years obsessively studying and drinking Champagne, I can assure you that Champagne is even better—way better—than you think it is. Not only that, but the personal journey of exploring Champagne, of discovering your own preferences and creating your own model of Champagne, is itself thrilling and satisfying. That's the great news. The problem is that there is no guide for your expedition. You could explore Champagne the way I did: by poring over numerous dense reference books, taking long instructional courses, stumbling through Champagnes you don't understand for reasons you don't understand, compiling hundreds of tasting notes and trying to find threads and distinctions here and there. At the same time, if you take that path, you'll need to do even more research to figure out what parts of Champagne marketing and promotion are true and helpful and what other parts are false, misleading, and misguided. Sounds fun, right?

Hell no. I wrote this book because there is another way, an easier way, and I want to share it with you. You can know and enjoy Champagne as much as I do. To accomplish this, you don't need to be a wine expert, or memorize every bit of minutiae about Champagne, or have a specially trained palate, or consume hundreds of bottles of wine. Nor do you need a hyper-specific instructional manual, as if you were assembling an Ikea bedroom set.

What you need is a guide. A guide does not tell you exactly what to think, what to like, or what to do. A guide points out the noteworthy and, by doing so, helps you find your own path. That is what this book is. I'm going to show you how to organize your journey through Champagne, what to look for, and how to understand what you encounter. You just need to bring your curiosity, your willingness to explore mindfully, and your love of Champagne. If you do that, at the end of it, you will have opened the doors to the amazements in Champagne and will have become a better, more satisfied, more joyful Champagne drinker. And who in their right mind wouldn't want that?

We're going on an adventure through Champagne. And we're doing it with purpose. So grab a glass and an ice bucket, and get ready to drink and enjoy.

CHAPTER I

Champagne, Essentially

SOMEWHERE BETWEEN THE SELF-SATISFIED COLLECTOR of wine trivia and the person who knows very little about wine is a platform we need to stand on if we truly are to enjoy Champagne. We need to know enough about the fundamentals of Champagne to explore, understand, and differentiate bottles of Champagne. This is where the journey to drinking Champagne well—today and for the long term—begins.

What Champagne Is and Is Not

The French word *Champagne* resides in the working vocabulary of English speakers. If you told just about any adult that you drank Champagne last night, it's unlikely that the person would have no idea what you were talking about. And yet, if you ask enough people what Champagne is or where it is from, or if you listen carefully to the way the word is used and misused, it becomes obvious that many of us are not quite certain what Champagne is and what it is not. To be clear, Champagne is: (1) the name of a particular wine region in France; and (2) the name of a sparkling wine made in the Champagne wine region, in accordance with the rules in that region. Champagne is not: (1) a generic name for sparkling wine—a wine that is bubbly because it contains sufficient carbon dioxide; or (2) a generic term indicating a luxury product.

1

The point is made sharply in a large banner on every page of the website of the Comité Champagne, the trade association that represents grape growers and wine producers in Champagne: "Champagne only comes from Champagne, France." That's all there is to it. Almost.

The purpose of the "Champagne only comes from Champagne, France" campaign is to avoid consumer confusion, whether caused by mistakes or intentional rip-offs. Champagne is by far the most valuable, prestigious, historical brand in the world of sparkling wine, but Champagne accounts for only around 10% of worldwide sparkling wine production. It's a situation that makes some confusion inevitable. Almost every wine drinker has suffered the distinctly disappointing experience of having been offered "Champagne" by a person who, not knowing any better, pours a glass of the world's best-*selling* sparkling wine, Prosecco.* To prevent wine producers from misleading consumers and capitalizing on the possibility of confusion, the laws of most countries prohibit the use of the word "Champagne" on sparkling wines that are not, in fact, Champagne. European law even prohibits anyone outside of Champagne from claiming to make sparkling wine by the *méthode champenoise* (the generic terms *méthode traditionnelle* or *méthode classique* may be used instead).

Unfortunately, when lawmakers in the United States have had to choose between drinkers' interest in honest labels and the wine industry's interest in making money, they too often have sided with industry. Prior to 2006, wine-labeling laws in the United States allowed the California wine industry to masquerade as an Epcot World Pavilion of wine—producers

* The subtitle of this book is "A Guide to Enjoying the World's Greatest Sparkling Wine." I am confident that the consensus view of those who would know is that, as a category, Champagne is the world's best. And in any event, that's what I think and what you think. But it's noteworthy that there are many great sparkling wines made outside of Champagne, which this book does not cover. There also are many cheap and substandard bottles of Champagne (mostly sold in supermarkets in France and the UK) that merit no discussion in a book about Champagne.

of mostly inexpensive, crappy wines magically created Burgundy, Chablis, Port, and, naturally, "California Champagne." That ended, for the most part, with a 2006 federal law that bars the importation or bottling of wine that is labeled as "Champagne" but is not from Champagne. But the law grandfathered in producers who had been using approved labels prior to March 10, 2006. This means that brands such as Korbel, Cook's, and André, which sold wines labeled "California Champagne" prior to that date, are permitted to continue with this ridiculous, deceptive scheme. I'm all in favor of a boycott, especially since there are many excellent California sparkling wines from producers who don't feel the need to take a free ride on Champagne's name.*

Before we leave the topic of what is not Champagne, it's important to recognize that, in some sense, Champagne is not really Champagne. That is, the image that the Champagne industry has crafted for itself, the stories it tells, and the claims it makes about its wines do not always align with the truth. They exist only because they *do* align with the goal of selling as much Champagne as possible at the greatest possible prices.

As an example, perhaps the best-known story in Champagne is that of the monk Dom Pérignon. But the story has been revised so significantly over time that, at this point, there are now *two* Dom Pérignons. The first is the actual, historical Benedictine monk who was the cellar master of the Abbey of Hautvillers about 300 years ago. This real Dom Pérignon made excellent wines that were highly regarded in his time, particularly still white wines made from black grapes. He developed important advances in viticulture and winemaking, for which he deserves great credit. But there is no reliable evidence that

---

* Other commercial misappropriations of Champagne's brand equity may be pathetic but are not necessarily a concern for the Champagne drinker. For example, over one hundred years ago, the Miller Brewing Company began advertising that its High Life beer was "The Champagne of Bottled Beer." In 1969, the catchier "The Champagne of Beers" emerged, a moniker that adorns bottles to this day. At this point, with so many high-quality beers in the market, it's kind of embarrassing.

he intentionally made sparkling wine. To the contrary, it is most likely that Dom Pérignon (like his contemporaries in Champagne) believed effervescence to be a wine flaw.

The second Dom Pérignon is a mostly fictional character invented in the 19th century and smartly appropriated by Moët & Chandon in the 1930s as the name of its prestige cuvée. Unlike the real monk, this Dom Pérignon is blind, presumably to emphasize his remarkable sense of taste. Not only does this blind monk make sparkling wine, but he actually invents it, calling out to his associate, "Come quickly, I am tasting the stars!" And here is the best part, where historical fantasy makes the leap into corporate reality: Dom Pérignon's fictional sparkling Champagne apparently continues to be made today by the French luxury goods conglomerate LVMH Moët Hennessy Louis Vuitton. Indeed, LVMH claims on its website that Dom Pérignon Champagne has a "creation date" of 1668 (the year the real Dom Pérignon arrived at the Abbey of Hautvillers and became its cellar master) and that the current Dom Pérignon brand "perpetuates" the historical monk's "vision and work." Perhaps the company's marketing department has convinced itself that these statements don't cross into hazardous territory. But let's be real. At the very least, LVMH appears to be suggesting that it can meaningfully trace the lineage of its Dom Pérignon Champagne to wines made by the most famous historical figure in Champagne. And for all intents and purposes, that it is not true.

Why am I raining on LVMH's parade on account of what arguably is a harmless fairy tale? The moral and practical reasons for telling the truth are familiar. But more specifically, for the person who genuinely wants to explore, understand, and enjoy Champagne, the road is made more hazardous when Champagne-industry professionals choose to litter it with lies, bullshit, irrelevant information, and relevant omissions. And it's all so unnecessary. The actual facts about who makes Champagne, how they make it, how various styles and brands differ from one another, and how the wines taste, are compelling. We truly are living in a golden age of Champagne, in which drinkers have access to a broader array of diverse, high-quality wines, sold at different price points, than ever before. We should be celebrating *that* Champagne—the *true* Champagne. To start, we will take a look at what really makes Champagne special today: the place, the people, and the wines.

The Place

A few years ago, I told a very smart friend that I had made plans to visit Champagne. She laughed dismissively, "There is no place called Champagne." This was an impressive example of a person being right in such a limited and unimportant way as to make the person wrong.

Before the French Revolution, Champagne was the name of a province in northeast France, and it was well known for its excellent wines. But the French disposed of romantic provinces in favor of bureaucratic departments, which led to a succession of further bureaucratic tinkering with names and boundaries. In 1956, most of the area in which Champagne is made became part of the French administrative region of Champagne-Ardenne, which comprised four departments: Ardennes, Aube, Haute-Marne, and Marne. In 2016, the government reduced the number of administrative regions, for whatever reason, and combined Champagne-Ardenne with the adjoining regions of Alsace and Lorraine to form the new, larger Grand Est administrative region. I suppose if you want to be politically accurate, whenever you decide to visit the place in France where Champagne is made, you could tell your friends and family, "I'm going to Grand Est this summer!" To be comprehensive, you might mention you will tour portions of Hauts-de-France and Île-de-France.

Or you could just say you're going to Champagne. That's because Champagne is a legally delimited wine region in France. It is, with various additions and subtractions, basically where the old Champagne province was located. But the Champagne wine region is different from any political subdivision, in that it is a patchwork of non-contiguous areas that are approved for the growing of grapes, the production of Champagne, or both. Technically, there are three legal components to the region that relate to the making of Champagne: a larger area of land covering more than 600 communes in which Champagne can be made (the *Zone de l'Élaboration*); the smaller area within that zone consisting of 319 villages that are entitled to grow grapes for Champagne (the *Zone de Production*); and the specific places within these villages where vineyards may be planted with grapes that can be used to make Champagne (the *Zone Parcellaire de Production de Raisins*).

For the wine drinker, the first zone doesn't matter much, other than to know that, again, a sparkling wine not made in this region is not Champagne. But the second and third zones might matter when we decide to buy or drink a bottle of Champagne. As discussed in Chapter 6, in some cases we might want to know the name of the village, and perhaps the vineyard, where grapes were grown for our bottle of Champagne. That's because Champagne's vineyard areas are spread out and differently situated, leading to differences in wines. As a point of reference, the map at the end of this book shows a high-level overview of the Champagne vineyard areas, the subregions of Champagne, the main two cities, and the seventeen Grand Cru villages.

Champagne is situated in the north of France, and that location points to the single most important natural factor that makes Champagne an ideal place to produce great sparkling wine: climate. Champagne's vineyards are located at around the 48th parallel in the southern part of the region and above the 49th parallel in the north. This puts the vineyards near the northern limit of where it is possible to successfully grow wine grapes. Average annual temperatures are around 52°F, which is very cold for a wine region. This is ideal for growing grapes to be used for sparkling wine. The basic reason is that grapes (the right grapes, discussed below) can ripen over the growing season while retaining the high levels of acidity and lower levels of potential alcohol that are necessary to make outstanding sparkling wine. In warmer climates without significant cooling influences, sparkling wines can be too high in alcohol and too low in acidity, resulting in wines that are flabby, not refreshing, and, frankly, gross.*

Champagne is blessed with a climate that usually (but not every year) provides not only cold temperatures but also sunny summers and enough rain throughout the year to support grape growing, without the high levels of rain that could damage grapes or ruin harvests. Of course, this is not to say that Champagne is free of climatic challenges. In any given year, Champagne is subject to potentially devastating frosts, hail, humidity, lack of sun, or too much rain at the wrong times. This variability creates differences in vintage wines made in different years, as discussed in Chapter 4. But the important point is that Champagne maintains a significant natural advantage over other sparkling wine regions by virtue of its climate. This is one of the main reasons the best sparkling wines from other wine regions do not, as a whole, measure up to the best sparkling wines from Champagne.

At least, that's true today. If you need another reason to procure cases of Champagne right now in preparation for the apocalyptic future of your choosing, it is this: climate change. Different grape varieties ripen over different periods of time. Champagne is made almost exclusively from three varieties that ripen relatively early. This is advantageous for the reason mentioned above: in a cold climate, these grapes will see an extended growing season; they can be harvested when they are just ripe in late summer or early fall, when they still have high acidity and moderate

---

* High acidity is a prominent feature of Champagne that I will discuss through-out this book. Many wine drinkers appreciate the effect of acidity in wine, but for everyone else, the basic idea is that acidity is refreshing. It makes your mouth water (re-fresh) after you have swallowed or spit out a sufficiently acidic liquid. Generally, the higher the acidity, the more your mouth waters. To test this, take in a mouthful of pure lemon juice and swirl it around; then spit it out into the sink. Notice that you are drooling uncontrollably. That's high acidity.

potential alcohol. Climate change threatens to destroy this balance. Over the last three decades, grapes have ripened more quickly in Champagne, resulting in lower acidity and higher potential alcohol. So far, this development hasn't been so bad for Champagne and may even have helped. Winemakers have been able to employ techniques to adjust for the warming climate, and Champagne has avoided the historical problem of not being able to ripen grapes in very cold years. But think of our kids and the potential of a disastrous future in which they can't enjoy great Champagne! Seriously, if we don't do something about climate change soon, all of our current wine books will become nothing more than historical curiosities, including this one.

Looking back to the map, what can else can we say about the geographic area of Champagne that is material to the wine? Notice when you view the map as a whole that vineyard areas are spread out, disconnected, and dispersed unevenly over a large area. What the map doesn't show is that vineyards also are planted at different aspects to the sun and, to a much lesser extent, altitudes. The most significant effect of these differences is that the region is home to innumerable microclimates. As a consequence, each of Champagne's grape varieties grows better or worse than the others in different areas and, more to the point of this book, grow *differently* in various places, which is one cause of the diversity of wines in Champagne. This connection between vineyard locations in Champagne and the diversity of wines available to be explored is taken up in Chapter 6.

Champagne's ideal macroclimate and its diverse microclimates are perhaps the most obvious environmental factors that influence the character of the region's wines. But no book about Champagne should fail to mention a third natural factor that often draws more attention than the others: soil, and specifically, chalk. Champagne is said to have a natural advantage because vast vineyard areas are situated over a bedrock of chalk. There is some truth to this. Chalk is a very porous type of limestone that is ideal for regulating the amount of water available to vines; it drains well during heavy rainfall so as to avoid waterlogging but also stores water that vines can use when they need it. This works hand in hand with Champagne's climate, making Champagne special. Champagne growers and producers care about the composition of soil underneath vineyards, because distinct soil types and structures can suggest the growing of one grape variety instead of another, the employment of particular viticultural practices, and the selection of grapes to be used for wines.

The question, though, is whether the Champagne drinker should care about chalk when making buying or drinking decisions. Should we survey Champagne in search of wines from vineyards that have more chalk, deeper chalk, superior chalk? I believe the answer is no. In the first place, the Champagne vineyards are located in a wide array of mixtures of various soils, and there is no evidence that there is one best soil composition, let alone a direct relationship between the amount or purity of chalk and the quality of wine.

More importantly, here again it is wise for consumers to ignore marketing from certain corners of the Champagne industry. Some insist that chalk not only supports good vine health but also directly influences the taste of a wine in specific ways, making Champagne "mineral" or, more outlandishly, "chalky." These kinds of claims lack any rational basis. Chalk (calcium carbonate) has no flavor and is not, in any event, taken up through the roots of vines, stored in grapes, or processed into wine. If chalky soil has any effect on the flavor of wine, we don't know either the effect or the mechanism. But if nature loves to hide, as Heraclitus observed, it's also true that industry loves to market. Bollinger makes the bizarre claim on its website that chalk "has a lifelike quality," while Veuve Clicquot's website asserts, as if it were a provable fact, that chalky soil gives Champagne "its mineral notes." My point here is that paying attention to certain claims about Champagne is more likely to cause confusion than understanding. At the very least, it is fair to say that the Champagne industry has elevated the discussion of chalk way out of proportion to its potential importance. Overall, when investigating (*i.e.*, buying and drinking) Champagne, I believe it's best for you to ignore soils and any claim made about them.

Perhaps this discussion of chalk is a good place to point out a paradox in wine: you can't enjoy a wine without knowing it, but attempting to know a wine can prevent its enjoyment. The key is to figure out what in the material world of wine matters and what doesn't, and then to experience the wine on your own terms. Place does matter in Champagne for the reasons mentioned, and in any other ways it does not. Of course, sparkling wine doesn't make itself in Champagne, which brings us to the people of Champagne, the Champenois.

The People

We tend to think of the people in a wine region along two dimensions. The first is the captivating question of what those who grow grapes and make wines are like as human beings. This is true of anyone we regard as an artisan in any field. We imagine that the more we know about the elderly Japanese blacksmith in Sanjo—his family history, his upbringing, his personality—the more we will not merely understand, but also love and revere, the tool that he made with his hands and is now in ours. The focus can be pulled back to the entire region to explore the product through the social and cultural history of the people who make it. Wine adds the element of nostalgia for a simpler agrarian lifestyle that most of us have never experienced but that nevertheless provokes longing. Wine journalism and wine marketing lean heavily on this first dimension. This is not surprising. Human-interest stories are fascinating, and they sell product. Champagne, in particular, has a rich cultural history and enough intriguing contemporary personalities to fill several books already written.

But for the person who wants to explore Champagne's wines, focusing the lens on specific people and personalities, or pulling back to make generalizations about the Champenois as a whole, sometimes can be more misleading than informative. In large part this is because the Champagne industry is very diverse and complex, and it's almost impossible to make relevant generalizations about it that are material to any particular wine. Much of the wine production is carried out by large companies, though there are many smaller producers and co-operatives as well. And among the thousands of grape growers, the ranges of size, quality, and other characteristics are wide. To try to draw durable conclusions about wines by divvying up people in Champagne based on who they appear to be in a glossy profile is misguided at best. I will have more to say about this in Chapter 3, in which we examine producers of various sizes, but the fact is that great wines—and in many cases similar wines—are made in Champagne by producers of all shapes, sizes, and personalities.

A second, much more helpful, way of understanding the people of Champagne is to view them through the lens of the mechanics of production. In other words, to focus on what the various people and organizations in a region actually do and how they do it. Knowing something about who is involved in making a particular bottle of Champagne and what they do can help us understand what is in a wine and meaningfully discriminate between wines.

The Champagne industry historically has been divided into two groups, though they overlap significantly: those who make sparkling wine and those who grow grapes for sparkling wine. There are approximately 360 Champagne houses, which collectively sell Champagne under more than 1,000 different brand names. These include well-known houses such as Bollinger, Moët & Chandon, Mumm, Pol Roger, and Veuve Clicquot. The legal designation for a Champagne house is *Négociant Manipulant,* and every bottle of Champagne sold by a house will contain the letters NM and an identification number in small print.

An NM is entitled to make Champagne from its own grapes, from grapes grown by others in Champagne, or from both. These houses sell more than 70% of all Champagne, and they exert an even greater influence in the export market. For example, approximately 88% of all Champagne imported into the United States comes from one of the Champagne houses.

Despite their dominance over the market for wines, the houses own only about 10% of the vineyard land in Champagne. The other 90% is owned by almost 16,000 independent grape growers, who mostly sell their grapes to the houses. Even Moët, which owns almost 3,000 acres of vines, needs to buy a lot of grapes from growers to have enough material to make its wines. The grape growers would be mostly invisible to consumers, except that some of them also sell small volumes (compared to the large houses) of wine that they make from their own grapes. As we will see, making Champagne for sale is an expensive, complicated, and risky enterprise. Therefore, most growers who do make wine also sell a portion of their grapes to houses to generate relatively steady income. The term *Récoltant Manipulant* (RM on a bottle) generally refers to a grower-producer who makes Champagne under its own label solely from grapes it farms.* Most RMs sell their wines only in France or other countries in Europe, and fewer than 200 sell into the United States. About 6% of Champagne sold in the U.S. is made by RMs.

In Chapter 3, I delve deeper into the issue of houses and growers, and the popular but false idea that grower Champagne is, by definition, better or more praiseworthy than Champagne made by the houses. For now, know that the lines have been blurred enough that you can't just

---

* There are enterprising Champenois who use legal loopholes to make wines labeled RM or NM that really should not be labeled as such if the spirit of the law were followed. I suppose Grover Cleveland was right that "no man has ever yet been hanged for breaking the spirit of a law," but, damnit, we're talking about Champagne! Anyway, it's relatively rare to encounter these wines outside of Europe, and this book does not mention them.

blindly toss bottles marked NM into the "non-grower" bin. For one thing, several of the most celebrated makers of grower Champagne have turned in their RM badges to become NMs—and not because they decided to join the dark side or stop making grower Champagne. They did so simply because they need access to a certain volume of high-quality grapes from other growers to supplement their own, and buying additional expensive vineyard land in Champagne often is not economically feasible. On the other hand, some NMs sell what can only be called grower Champagne. For example, Louis Roederer is a large NM, and it does buy grapes for some of its wines. But all of its vintage Champagnes are made exclusively from Roederer's own vineyards. And then there is Dehours, an outstanding family-owned grower estate that happens to be registered as an NM but doesn't buy any grapes to make its wines. The bottom line is that the bottle code NM will tell you that a producer can purchase grapes, but it won't tell you that a bottle of wine actually contains purchased grapes.

Although there are five other legally recognized categories for Champagne producers, the only other one you are likely to encounter outside of Costco* is *Coopérative de Manipulation* (CM). Cooperatives allow grape growers who individually lack the financial resources to make and sell Champagne to do so collectively. Around seventy Champagne cooperatives pool grapes from their members and sell Champagne under the cooperatives' labels. The most significant cooperative is Nicolas Feuillatte, which is one of the largest producers of Champagne and is

---

* Costco's Kirkland line of wines (including Champagne) is a type of brand that is unusual in the United States but common in parts of Europe, where many supermarkets and restaurants sell what are referred to as "private label" or "buyer's own brand" wines. In that scheme, a winemaker produces wine for the buyer and labels it with the buyer's brand instead of the winemaker's. In Champagne, the designation for that type of arrangement is *Marque d'Acheteur,* and you will see the letters MA on Kirkland Champagne. I would hate for the first description of a specific wine in this book to leave an overall negative impression, so I will just say that everyone should try Kirkland Champagne at least once.

responsible for a very large proportion of CM Champagne imported in the United States.

Finally, it's important to recognize that the grape growers and wine producers do not act completely independently in making Champagne. They are, of course, bound by certain rules established by the French government. But on a local level, they also act collectively to make and enforce rules concerning the production and sale of Champagne, to conduct research and experiments to improve Champagne, and to market and protect the Champagne brand. These collective actions by the Champenois have a significant effect on the wine that ends up in your glass. Much of the work is carried out by a joint trade association of growers and producers, which also has a certain amount of regulatory authority from the French government, known as the Comité Champagne. The Comité Champagne maintains a website in English that, while predictably overly exuberant and imperfect, contains a good deal of useful information for wine drinkers.

Now that we know something about where Champagne is and who is involved in making it, it's time to get to know the main attraction: the wine.

The Wine

When you look at a glass of Champagne, one feature stands out immediately: bubbles. The funny thing about bubbles is that some of them, the ones that seem frivolous, make us happy. There must be something very human about that, some reason why children instinctively take pleasure in bubbles in soap or gum, why adults laugh at these kinds of bubbles too, why we like to put bubbles of gas inside thin plastic to make balloons. Unquestionably, this phenomenon explains part of the joy we draw from Champagne. It is the reason Champagne is poured into flutes, which are terrible wine-drinking vessels, but which facilitate a long, dense stream of bubbles better than other glasses. We have the impulse to hold up a glass, look at the bubbles, and smile. One thing we can say about the bubbles in Champagne—no matter how expensive or profound a particular wine may be—is that they are capable of providing amusement. Frankly, a denial of this fact is the start of cutting the human being out of the Champagne drinking experience.

But bubbles in Champagne also serve a purpose opposite to playfulness; they perform a serious function in the wine. Critically, bubbles change the texture of wine in the mouth, and the amount and character of the bubbles affect how Champagne feels when you are drinking it. A lot of attention is paid to how wines smell or taste—with "taste" generally referring to flavor. Less emphasis is given to texture—how a wine feels in the mouth. Texture significantly influences how we experience a wine as a whole, given all of its other components. In quality wines, textural elements, such as the bubbles in Champagne, are not just hanging out in a liquid to do their own thing; they are designed to work in harmony with other elements. Taste two glasses of the same good-quality Champagne, one served with bubbles and one flat, and you will experience a difference that goes beyond mouthfeel as a separate component. The flat Champagne will not only seem less lively but also imbalanced and disjointed. It's missing something important that a wine intentionally made still is not. Once you begin to notice them, it's easy to see that bubbles in Champagne serve a purpose that is not at all frivolous but rather essential to character and quality.

And, as it turns out, not all bubbles are created equal. Bubbles are a good jumping-off point to something important about Champagne that partially answers the question of why we should care to know Champagne more than we would other sparkling wines: Champagne is made the hard way, the expensive way, the time-consuming way, through processes designed at every stage to maximize quality. In the 21st century, it's very easy to get bubbles into wine. Inject carbon dioxide under pressure into wine and, *voilà*, bubbles. A tremendous amount of sparkling wine is made in just this way, and you could probably do it at home. But in Champagne, as described in more detail below, bubbles are created by encouraging wine to ferment a second time inside a bottle, and trouble is taken to keep the bubbles in the bottle during a process in which dead yeast cells are later removed from the wine. The result is a softer, more integrated, more persistent mousse in your glass of Champagne than you will find in cheaply made sparkling wines. The effort it takes to produce Champagne, the complexity of the process, and the quality that results make Champagne worth knowing.

Beyond appreciating that Champagne is a wine engineered for quality, it's important for the Champagne explorer to have a basic understanding of the steps of production. This is because even though the steps are regulated, bound at the edges by certain rules, they also allow for a wide array of choices by the winemaker. Some of these choices affect quality, others affect diversity, and others make no difference other than in marketing materials. Throughout this book, I will point to wines in which different choices were made in the first and second categories, and this is the key to differentiating Champagnes when you drink them.

Step 1: Harvesting grapes

I'll start by mostly skipping the beginning. The first step in making Champagne, of course, is to grow and harvest grapes. There are rules to be followed and choices to be made here, but I cover this subject in Chapter 2, where we dive into the different grape varieties used to make Champagne. For now, the basic piece of information to know is that almost all Champagne is made from one or more (and usually at least two) of three grape varieties: Chardonnay, Pinot Noir, and Pinot Meunier.

What also should be noted is that grapes in Champagne play a slightly different role than they do in still wines and in most other sparkling wines. You'll sometimes hear makers of still wines assert, with superficial modesty, the primacy of grapes. They might say something like, "I let the grapes make wine themselves. I try to stay out of the way." It's as if what is going on is the foraging of grapes in the wild, once they have fallen to the earth, breaking their skins to expose juice to wild yeast, beginning an alcoholic fermentation of liquid that needs only to be collected and bottled. In reality, this nod to nature never captures the truth of wine-making, but the point is taken that the wine in your glass might be the purest expression of modern-day wine from a particular grape variety. The grape may not be alone on the stage, but it's spotlighted in the center.

In Champagne, the grape has company. Smell a good Champagne in a glass, and often one of the most notable characteristics will be a category of aromas that you might associate with a biscuit, dough, or bread. In almost any Prosecco, by contrast, you will smell none of these. The difference is that Champagne is put through a process of yeast autolysis, which, in combination with the other components in wine, can generate these aromas. Other aromas such as vanilla and toast can be caused by the Maillard reaction after sugar is introduced into a bottle of Champagne before bottling. What all of this means is that, in Champagne, for a wine to be elegant, interesting, complex, and balanced, grapes must be good teammates, complementing the various aromas and flavors that the process generates instead of trying to stand out front. This is why Champagne is made from grapes that are not highly aromatic but whose subtle flavors and high acidity play well with others.

Step 2: Pressing the grapes to obtain juice

The first process after harvesting is to press the grapes and extract juice. Pressing is one of the most consequential steps in the process of making Champagne, requiring expertise and thoughtfulness, though it's rarely a topic of marketing. The main reason pressing matters so much in Champagne is that, except in the case of a rosé (discussed in the next chapter), the objective is to separate, as much as possible, the clear juice inside grapes from the skins on the outside. Champagne is a white wine, so crushing black grapes (which make up the majority of grapes in Champagne) or even handling them roughly and letting the skins color the juice won't do. Plus, crushing the grapes could release bitter compounds into the juice, and that would be bad too.

For these reasons, good pressing really starts, in effect, in the vineyard, where whole clusters of grapes from vines are placed in small crates, so that the skins do not break and bleed juice on them. We don't yet have machines that can reliably harvest intact clusters, so grape clusters must be removed from vines by hand. These clusters are taken to a press house, where 4,000 kilograms of grapes are placed in a press, which separates the juice from the rest of the grape. Only the first 2,550 liters of juice pressed from this weight of grapes can be used to make Champagne. And of that, the first 2,050 liters that comes from the press is called the *cuvée*, and next 500 is called the *taille*. You might hear Champagne producers say that they only use the *cuvée*, which generally makes better Champagne.

A few producers go even further and claim to use only a middle portion of the *cuvée* for a wine—presumably the best of the best—and label it *Coeur de Cuvée* (heart of the *cuvée*). Vilmart, for example, makes such a wine from 1,400 liters of the *cuvée*—leaving out the first 150 liters (they just might have dragged in impurities as they dripped over grape skins) and the last 500 liters (they're dangerously close to the *taille*). It's a delicious Champagne, though it's impossible to tell how much of its deliciousness is due to this center cut of juice.

Step 3: Make base wines

With juice in hand, it's time to make wine. This is accomplished in more or less the same way it is everywhere: put grape juice in a vessel, add yeast (and sometimes sugar), and you get wine. In Champagne, though, this wine is not made to be drunk. Instead, it's an intermediate product, a base wine, of about 11% alcohol that is later converted into a higher-alcohol sparkling wine.

There are two factors at this stage of making Champagne that are worth mentioning. The first is the choice of the kind of vessel used to make wine. Most base wines are made in stainless-steel tanks, but some producers ferment all or a portion of their base wines in oak. Very few of these oak barrels are new, because the flavors that new oak can impart to a wine, such as coconut and cedar, generally are not considered desirable in Champagne. Instead, previously used oak barrels that will not add flavor are sometimes employed both for fermentation and storage of base wines to allow for small amounts of oxygen to enter the wine. This can affect the texture and aromas in a Champagne, and we will explore some wines that show this effect in Chapter 4.

The second factor is the winemaker's choice of whether to encourage or block a process called malolactic conversion. Grapes in Champagne tend to have a relatively high proportion of malic acid (think biting into a green apple), which sometimes can result in wines that seem overly tart. This is why most Champagne producers encourage bacteria to convert malic acid into lactic acid (think milk), giving wines a slightly softer, creamier texture. On the other hand, there is a growing trend in Champagne of blocking malolactic conversion. The advocates for this approach usually argue that it allows pure fruit character to show more clearly and makes wines seem fresher and brighter. They also point out that climate change has caused a decrease in levels of acidity in Champagne grapes. They believe that malolactic conversion is now unnecessary and counterproductive. Other producers fall somewhere in the middle, blending their Champagnes to have a proportion of wines that have gone through malolactic conversion. Others block the process in some years but not others, or in wines made from some vineyards and not others. And there are other producers who say they have no idea whether their wines go through malolactic conversion and don't care.

A Champagne producer's decision to allow or block malolactic conversion can make a difference in the way you experience a wine. This is not a winemaking choice that necessarily produces better or worse wines. I've yet to hear anyone say that they always drink, or always avoid, Champagne that has gone through malolactic conversion. What matters is how this choice affects particular wines, and I will demonstrate this in some examples as we go along.

Step 4: Blend wines

Champagne is almost always, in one way or another, a blended wine. Champagne producers typically make many different base wines separately every year. For example, the wines could be made from different grape varieties, or from grapes grown in different plots, vineyards, or villages. Wines from the same grape variety or vineyard could be fermented in different vessels, or they could be made in different ways. Not only that, but each year Champagne producers hold back a certain amount of wine to store as reserve wines for possible use in future years, and variances can be created in these wines by storing portions of them in different vessels. The end result of all of this is that a producer can create a blend with numerous different wines. As an example, Krug Grande Cuvée is made each year from a blend of more than a hundred separate wines from at least ten different years—and that's just the number actually used from the wines that are available to Krug. This doesn't mean that Krug Grand Cuvée tastes the same every year—it doesn't. But by having the ability to access so many wines, Krug can maintain a discernible house style, while also selecting for quality, harmony, and complexity.

When you think about it, it's amazing what winemakers do in Champagne to create blends. They have to decide which wines to use in the blend, and in what proportion, and they also have to use their imaginations. The combination of wines they choose will not resemble the final Champagne after it goes through the additional processes discussed below. The Champagne that eventually is bottled will have more alcohol, different aromas and flavors, bubbles, a different mouthfeel, a reduced impact from acidity, and, in the vast majority of wines, an extra dose of sugar. So blending is a game of predictions, and you get to play it only once each year. This is where Champagne can go sideways, and it takes experts in the art of blending to get it right. Throughout this book, we will be looking at different blending options and how they play out in the glass.

Step 5: Make it sparkle

Have you ever heard the story of how Post-It notes were developed? They were an accident resulting from a failure. A scientist at 3M tried to create a very strong adhesive, but he messed up big time and instead created a reusable, low-tack adhesive. One of his colleagues decided this stuff worked really well as an anchor for his bookmark, and eventually the public loved it. Office cubicles haven't been the same since.

Sparkling wine was an accident too, hundreds of years ago, before anyone understood the mechanics of alcoholic fermentation. Some winemakers noticed that if they made and bottled their wines in cold winter temperatures, when they opened them the following spring, after the weather warmed, the wines would have bubbles. How strange. What these winemakers didn't understand was that cold temperatures made yeasts go dormant before they were able to consume all of the available grape sugar during fermentation, only to wake up in the spring and make more alcohol. A byproduct of alcoholic fermentation is carbon dioxide, but it dissolves in bottled wine, so you can't tell just by looking at a bottle that a fermentation has occurred inside. However, when you open that bottle and pour wine into a glass, you get the appearance of bubbles, which at first were considered a major flaw. But eventually, in the same way people took to Post-Its, wine drinkers thought, *Hey, we actually like bubbles in wine sometimes.* And that led to intentionally created sparkling wines and eventually to Champagne.

In Champagne, bubbles do not arrive through this seasonal cooling-and-warming process, now called the ancestral method of producing sparkling wine. Instead, bubbles are generated by a second, independent alcoholic fermentation. To the final blend of wines, the winemaker adds certain amounts of sugar, yeast, yeast nutrients, and bentonite or some other substance that will help the dead yeast cells clump together so that they can be removed from the wine later. This is called the *liqueur de tirage. Tirage* refers to the drawing off of wine from barrel into bottle, and it's at this point that the wine is bottled. All of the action from here on out takes place in the same bottle that you eventually will hold in your hands. Once wine and the *liqueur de tirage* are in a bottle and sealed with a cork or a crown cap, the yeast gets to work making wine a second time, increasing the alcohol content of the wine to about 12.5%. Only now, carbon dioxide is trapped in the bottle instead of being released into the atmosphere, as it was during the first fermentation. This second fermentation usually takes about a month to complete, although it can go faster or slower, depending on the cellar's temperature. At the end, we finally have a sparkling wine—just not one we can drink yet.

Step 6: Lees aging

Yeasts are a type of fungus that, much like the mother octopus, die after doing their job. Many sparkling wines made throughout the world—Prosecco for example—have no use for dead yeast cells, more commonly called lees. They are filtered out of the wine soon after bubbles are born. But in Champagne, yeast plays an important role in death, through a process called autolysis.

The biological process of yeast autolysis—the breakdown of a dead yeast cell by its own enzymes—is pretty interesting, if you're into that kind of thing. But the main effect of autolysis on Champagne is to give the wine aromas of biscuits, bread dough, or nuts, and these are sometimes referred to as "autolytic" aromas. It's important to keep in mind that the effect of autolysis on Champagne is not a steady advance. Autolysis starts not long after the end of fermentation, but it takes a while for it to have any noticeable effect; it can significantly affect a wine that has been aged on its lees for several years, and then it might have little or no effect after a decade. Autolysis is not like adding more of an ingredient in equal portions to a wine over time. A Champagne aged on its lees for two years should taste different from an otherwise identical Champagne aged on its lees for nine. But the differences will be in the overall impressions of complexity, harmony, and flavor, which might not be so easily categorized. And more lees aging is not necessarily better. It's very possible that, for your palate, a Champagne aged for a very long period of time on its lees may seem heavy and unbalanced. Lees aging is something to get to know personally by drinking different Champagnes.

Fundamentally, autolytic notes are part of the character of Champagne, even if they are found only in small doses in certain wines. For this reason, French law requires Champagne to be aged on its lees for at least twelve months.* But most Champagne is aged significantly longer than that, so that the effects of autolysis are noticeable in the final wine. Exactly when and how long a particular Champagne was aged on its lees is easily calculated when a producer provides the relevant information on the back label of its bottles or on its website. But many producers refuse to do this, which is something I get very worked up over, as you will see in Chapter 5.

---

* That's what everyone says anyway, but it's not quite right. French law states, "*Le dégorgement ne peut être effectué avant une période de douze mois à compter de la date de tirage période pendant laquelle les vins devront être en bouteille sans interruption.*" In rough English, "Don't take the lees out of the bottle until at least twelve months from the date you put wine with the liqueur de tirage inside the bottle." In other words, a producer doesn't have to wait for the second fermentation to be complete and lees aging to begin to start the twelve-month clock. But I quibble.

Step 7: Get the lees out of the bottle

Lees play a very important role in the development of Champagne, but we don't want them hanging around in our bottle when we are ready to drink. They make the wine cloudy with sediment that nobody wants in their glass of Champagne. The processes of riddling and disgorgement are the means of getting rid of the lees before a bottle of Champagne is sealed with a cork.

The first step in eliminating lees from a Champagne bottle—riddling—is designed to collect the lees near the top of the bottle. This isn't accomplished by merely turning the bottle upside down, because lees stick to the inside of bottles. Riddling essentially is the process of rotating a Champagne bottle in short, quick segments many times over a period of days or weeks, so that eventually the lees clump together in the neck of an inverted bottle. Originally, this was performed exclusively by hand by expert riddlers, who placed bottles in wooden racks called *pupitres*. Around fifty years ago, two French winemakers invented a machine, called a gyropalette, which automates this process. Today, the gyropalette is widely used throughout Champagne. Some small producers don't use a gyropalette for economic reasons. Other producers, though, don't use it so that they can brag to you they don't use it. They hope you will think that their Champagne is better or, if not better, at least artisanal. There is no rational reason to believe that hand riddling improves or changes the quality of a bottle of Champagne, and you should be skeptical of those who promote it.

Once the lees are in the bottle's neck, they must be disgorged—ejected from the bottle. This must be done carefully, because opening the bottle to remove the lees will cause the loss of some amount of carbon dioxide and wine, as well as the entry of oxygen into the bottle. Almost all disgorgement is performed by a machine, which does the job not only well but consistently, so that one bottle of Champagne is not different from the next one on the line. Sometimes disgorgement must be done by hand—for example, if a bottle has been sealed with a cork and staple instead of a crown cap. Once again, some producers occasionally will make a small spectacle of their decision to hand disgorge when they could have used a machine instead.*

In any case, before the bottle is sealed for the last time with a cork, there is one more thing to do.

Step 8: Top up the wine (and add sugar)

It's been a long time since sweet Champagne was all the rage, and now the vast majority of Champagne does not taste sweet at all, even though it does receive a small addition of sugar before the cork is inserted. The purpose of adding a certain amount of sugar to Champagne is to achieve balance in the wine and, secondarily, to promote the development of additional aromas. Sugar added to Champagne is called dosage, and it's common to express dosage in terms of grams of sugar per liter of wine. Thus, the back of a Champagne label might say, "Dosage: 6 g/l." If a bottle of Champagne does receive dosage, it is mixed with a small amount of wine that is used to top up each bottle of Champagne, called the *liqueur d'expédition* ("shipping liquor").

Whether sugar is added to a particular bottle of Champagne and, if it is, how much, is very consequential. The amounts of sugar that are added are quite small, but even minor differences in these amounts can significantly change how a Champagne tastes. Unfortunately, sugar has been so demonized recently (despite that human beings continue to consume massive quantities of it) that, in some circles, eliminating

---

* The process of removing lees from Champagne through riddling and disgorgement is required by French law, except for bottles smaller than 375ml or larger than 3,000ml. That's because tiny and large bottles are very difficult to riddle, although some producers do it anyway. What producers are permitted to do with these smaller and longer bottles is use what is called the transfer method, in which bottles are emptied into a pressurized tank, the lees are filtered out, and wine is poured back into bottles. One other difference in this process is that, since wines from different bottles are mixed in a tank, the wine that ultimately is poured into a bottle will be just one portion of that mixture. Champagne in a 187ml split, for example, will have undergone the second fermentation in *a* bottle, but not *that* bottle.

dosage is more a matter of being in tune with fashion than actually enjoying Champagne. I will address dosage and its effects on different Champagnes in more detail in Chapter 4.

Step 9: Cork, rest, sell

With the final addition of the *liqueur d'expédition*, it's time to put a cork in the bottle, cover and secure the cork with a metal cage called the *muselet*, and—possibly—get the bottle out the door. I say "possibly" because, by law, Champagne may not leave a producer's cellar for at least fifteen months from the date of *tirage*—again, the bottling of the wine to start the second fermentation. As mentioned, a bottle cannot be disgorged until twelve months have elapsed from the date of *tirage*. If a producer disgorged a bottle of Champagne and gave it a cork at exactly the twelve-month point, it would need to lay the bottle down in its cellar for another three months of rest before selling it. But this rarely is an issue, because Champagne usually will be aged on its lees longer than fifteen months.

There is an additional aging requirement for what is called vintage Champagne. Vintage Champagne is a Champagne that is made entirely from grapes grown in one vintage year and that is labeled with the vintage year on the front of the bottle. If a producer wants to market a wine as a vintage Champagne, the bottle must rest in the producer's cellar for at least three years from the date of *tirage*. Here again, although a producer could leave a vintage wine on its lees for twelve months, disgorge and cork it, and then lay the bottle down for another two years, this is not what happens in the normal case. Vintage Champagnes most often are aged on their lees for several years, and this is part of the expected style of these wines. In Chapter 4, we will look at this difference between vintage and non-vintage Champagnes and how they can play out in a glass.

There you have it. Making a bottle of Champagne—especially a good one—takes considerable effort and expertise. And importantly for the drinker, there are numerous decisions to be made that offer innumerable possibilities. To take just a few examples: what grapes to use, from what vineyards, and in what proportions; whether to use reserve wines and, if so, which ones; how long to age a wine on its lees; whether to use dosage and the amount of dosage. These are some of the decision points that make for boundless diversity in Champagne. To my mind, this is what is so exciting about exploring Champagne.

Before we turn to the next chapter and discussions of particular wines, I should say a few things about the Champagnes discussed in this book. As I explained earlier, this book aims to be a useful guide for someone who wants to develop a personal understanding of Champagne through the first-person experience of drinking different wines. To this end, I have done my best to select Champagnes that are meaningfully illustrative and priced within what I believe is the sweet spot for value and quality in Champagne. I am not claiming that these are the best or most popular Champagnes. In fact, I have left out many of my favorites for various reasons. I chose the wines because they fit within the model I created to show you how to understand and explore Champagne. Like any model, this one is meant to be representative, and you could fill out the model differently with different Champagnes that would be just as useful. If you mindfully drink even a small fraction of the wines discussed in this book, you will develop a very good understanding of Champagne. And if you don't drink any of the Champagnes I have selected but instead use the discussions in the book to see how they resonate with your experience with other Champagnes, you can end up in the same place.

The vast majority of the wines discussed in this book retail in 2021 for between $40 and $125, with a high point of $200.* I have intentionally restrained myself from discussing very expensive Champagnes, for two reasons. First, you do not need to spend several hundred dollars or more to enjoy outstanding, expressive Champagne. Second, if you find yourself willing and able, for example, to spend over $2,000 for Krug Clos d'Ambonnay or Dom Pérignon P3, you really should not do so if you don't have a wide range of experience drinking less expensive Champagnes. It would be like getting a Porsche 911 Turbo for your 16th birthday. How are you supposed to appreciate it? The most expensive wine in this book is Louis Roederer Cristal. I wouldn't drink that first either.

A final point relates to the descriptions of wines in this book. Modern wine writing heavily favors deconstruction. If you read wine books written even thirty years ago, you are unlikely to find descriptions of wines having aromas of dried orange blossom, and baked yellow apple, and burnt nectarine peel, and roasted cinnamon sticks, and on and on. The danger posed by the expert's use of exceedingly certain, explicit, cerebral descriptions is not that they may be inaccurate and therefore might lead the reader astray. The real risk of this approach is the possibility of subverting the experience of wonder and discovery, the experience of the implicit and the ambiguous. If you've ever stood in a museum and felt moved by a painting, only to have an expert nearby break it down into a series of mechanical processes, pigments, and symbols, you know

---

* These prices apply to recent vintages of vintage-designated Champagnes, as indicated on Wine-Searcher.com (which is the best resource I know of for finding retailers who have a wine you may want, in stock and ready to ship to you). For example, in the next chapter, I discuss Taittinger Comtes de Champagne Blanc de Blancs. Recent vintages, such as 2007 or 2006, will cost you about $125 or so. And if you buy either of those wines and open them right now, you will learn why Comtes de Champagne is a great wine. But if you want to explore older and more esteemed vintages, then supply and demand will require a great outlay. For example, the 2002 vintage of Comtes de Champagne currently retails at about $300, while the 1996 can be found for around $500. I don't believe it makes sense to spend this much money for these wines, unless you already have a strong grasp of Champagne.

what I mean. In older wine books, authors guided readers to wines, perhaps noting that one wine is "scented and fine," while another has a "lovely nose and a good rich taste."* It's as if these writers thought you might want to enjoy the personal, emotional, inexplicable experience of discovering the wines yourself.

I've attempted in this book to point out differences in types and styles of Champagnes, without unnecessarily layering expectations and short-circuiting your personal exploration. And I will show you the kinds of experiences—intellectual and emotional—that I have had with these Champagnes, not because I think your reaction to each Champagne always will be the same as mine, but because I believe that you can find what I have found somewhere in Champagne. I am sure I haven't calibrated this perfectly for every reader. Most importantly, I hope my models or descriptions won't matter once you actually start drinking Champagne. All that matters is your investigation and discovery of Champagne from your first-person point of view, by drinking it.

And now, in the next chapter, we will start our exploration of drinking Champagne with the fundamental material of wine: grapes.

---

* It's hard to imagine a writer today getting away with descriptions such as these of vintages of Château Latour, which appeared in Harry Waugh's *Bacchus on the Wing* (1966).

CHAPTER 2

Drinking, Part 1:
Playing with Grapes

We're about to obsess a little bit over three grape varieties, which make up over 99% of the plantings in Champagne: Chardonnay, Pinot Noir, and Pinot Meunier. But before we do, let's take a deep breath and relax. You don't need to be an expert in viticulture or the lifecycle, peculiarities, and tendencies of these grape varieties to appreciate and enjoy Champagne. Just take in the basics that I explain below and drink.

It's also a good idea to have some perspective about grape varieties in Champagne. For thousands of years, until the early 20th century, human beings enjoyed drinking wine without caring very much about grape varieties. This was as true in Champagne as anywhere. As we have seen, Champagne is a processed wine, which can diminish the significance of varietal character. And Champagne always has been overwhelmingly a blended wine, with multiple different grape varieties from different vineyards composing the blend. The focus in Champagne traditionally was on how winemakers could make the best wines from the plant materials available to them, as opposed to figuring out how to coax an expression from a single grape variety. In the first significant book on Champagne written in English, Henry Vizetelly, in 1882, delved deeply into the wines, but devoted exactly two paragraphs to a discussion of grape varieties. He briefly mentioned fourteen varieties by name, said little about them, and concluded by noting that there are "a half a score of others."

Nobody knows for sure why wine drinkers became fixated on grape varieties and their differences in the last hundred years. Personally, I blame French bureaucracy. In the early 20th century, France began regulating wine in ways that didn't merely protect winemakers and consumers from fraud; the government created regional and stylistic wine identities. One way that the government accomplished this was by limiting the grape varieties that could be used to make particular wines in particular places. This elevated the importance of grape varieties in the consumer's consciousness, and now everyone and their mother has a preference for Cabernet Sauvignon or Merlot.

I provide this context not to suggest that there is anything wrong with being curious about grape varieties but to ensure that our curiosity doesn't lead to tunnel vision. Even today most Champagnes, including most great Champagnes, are not single-varietal wines. They are blends of two or more of Chardonnay, Pinot Noir, and Pinot Meunier. These grapes are blended not so that each will stand out separately in a wine like a collection of parts, but so that they will work together to make something new and different—a compound instead of a mixture. As I have mentioned, blending is one of the great arts in Champagne. If we are hunting for grape identity in our Champagne blends, we may miss the point and, more importantly, the pleasure.

Yet, great single-varietal wines also are made in Champagne. And drinking these Champagnes is a good place to start. These wines not only are delicious, but they give us insight into what each of the three grapes of Champagne contribute to blends. After exploring these grapes individually, we will drink them as blends. Then we will drink rosé

Champagne, a category of Champagne that is variously misunderstood, underappreciated, overpriced, and profound.

Chardonnay

If you had to select one grape variety as the very best for making great sparkling wines, unquestionably it would be Chardonnay. In Champagne, Chardonnay is that friend you admire for all the right reasons. Modest but luminous, reserved at the appropriate times and eloquent from the first word, a team player who leads confidently whenever the circumstances command, she gets along with everyone and fits into just about every social situation. Chardonnay is a star in Champagne because it is capable of delivering everything you want Champagne to be: at times fresh, elegant, racy, powerful, light, creamy, drinkable young, drinkable old, the perfect aperitif, the perfect meal wine. Chardonnay is the cornerstone of Champagne.

There are three fundamental keys to Chardonnay's success in Champagne. First, Chardonnay is an early-ripening grape. In Champagne's cold climate, this means that Chardonnay will see a long, slow ripening season. At harvest, Chardonnay will be ripe but still high in acidity. High acidity—what causes Champagne to be mouthwatering and refreshing—is essential to Champagne's style and is delivered to blends in large part through Chardonnay. Second, Chardonnay's flavors and aromas are restrained, subtle, understated. This too is beneficial in Champagne because Chardonnay doesn't overwhelm the aromas and flavors from yeast autolysis (such as toast, pastries, dough); instead, it complements and augments them. By contrast, a very aromatic and distinctive grape variety, such as Sauvignon Blanc, would overpower or clash with autolytic notes. Finally, Chardonnay is capable of making wines that are outstanding when young but that also can age into more complex, more interesting wines. You only have to look south to Burgundy to see this in action. Chardonnay gives Champagne drinkers who hold on to their wines for many years something to look forward to.

In Champagne, you will not see the word "Chardonnay" on the front of a bottle. Instead, a Champagne that is made entirely from white grapes may be labeled *blanc de blancs* ("white of whites"). Legally, it is permissible to include in a *blanc de blancs* one or more of three other white grape varieties: Arbane, Petit Meslier, and Pinot Blanc. But today these grapes are planted in such small quantities in Champagne that they are rarely used. Almost all *blanc de blancs* in Champagne are made exclusively from Chardonnay. Let's dive into six of these wines and see what Chardonnay can do.

RUINART BLANC DE BLANCS

Still wine has been made in Champagne for well over a thousand years, but it wasn't practical or desirable to produce sparkling wine on a large scale until the early 18th century. The floodgates were opened by a royal decree in 1728, which permitted wine to be shipped in bottle (instead of by cask only)—obviously necessary if one is going to ship a sparkling wine without losing carbon dioxide. This led to the establishment in 1729 of the first Champagne house devoted to making sparkling wine: Ruinart. Today, Ruinart is highly regarded for its attention to Chardonnay, and it produces a truly benchmark non-vintage *blanc de blancs* that is a perfect starting point for exploring this style.

Ruinart Blanc de Blancs shows Chardonnay at its friendliest. It's ripe, soft, plush, and fruity, with a dose of toastiness. It's so creamy that you start to believe you can smell creaminess. There are no sharp edges in the wine. It's a prime example of what happens in Champagne when a producer selects ripe Chardonnay, ensures malolactic conversion, and avoids oxidation. Importantly, notice too that this wine is fresh and lively, with mouthwatering acidity. It's the harmony of these elements that make Ruinart Blanc de Blancs such a drinkable, popular wine. The term "easy drinking" is thrown around with wines like this because it is easily, immediately pleasing. You can serve it any time of day to anyone—people who love Champagne, people who don't, experts, novices, whomever. It's a people pleaser.

While we're here, I must say that Ruinart does something very, very bad: it places this delicious wine in a clear glass bottle, just for show. Champagne normally is bottled in amber or green glass to protect it from light. "Light strike" happens when light from the environment interacts with amino acids in wine, transforming them into awful-smelling compounds. You only need to smell onions, cabbage, or sewage in Champagne once to be outraged by clear bottles. Ruinart is aware of the issue, explaining that "Ruinart Blanc de Blanc bottles are made from transparent glass intentionally to highlight the Chardonnay, but the wine should be stored away from any natural or artificial light source." Putting sparkling wine in a clear bottle is like speeding in a school zone—it's unnecessary and selfish; while the risk of harm may be small, the potential consequences are catastrophic. It's disappointing that such a beautiful wine is treated this way. Until Ruinart stops playing a game of chicken with this Champagne, I suggest keeping it in a bag. Still, Ruinart Blanc de Blancs is a building block for understanding Chardonnay in Champagne because it is a quality wine, right down the middle of the mainstream. It's a gateway and a point of reference from which you can compare so many other *blanc de blancs* and find your bearings.

Louis Roederer Blanc de Blancs

When I was in college, I veered over to the school of the arts to take a year-long course in music history. My professor loved music of all kinds and styles, and he praised numerous composers for various reasons. When we got to J.S. Bach, however, he wanted to be crystal clear about one point: Bach was a "hundred percenter"; he only wrote music of the highest quality. It's quite a statement, and I've thought about it in many contexts since.

In my opinion, there is a house in Champagne that is a "hundred percenter"—Louis Roederer. Roederer famously makes Cristal, but what many people don't know is that Roederer is relentless in its pursuit of quality and improvement at every level of production and for every type of Champagne it produces. In an age when large conglomerates buy and sell Champagne houses, swap out management teams, and vary houses' styles based on the way the winds blow, Roederer has been in the hands of the same family for 200 years. What you get in a glass of Louis Roederer Champagne is the product of a commitment to the preservation of legacy and a quest to improve on what came before. Among other things, Roederer owns more biodynamically farmed vineyards than anyone else in Champagne, is alone among Champagne houses in owning a nursery for the research and development of its vines, and separately vinifies wine from more than 400 different parcels. This kind of care, attention, and drive finds its results in the bottle. Every bottle of Louis Roederer Champagne is in the top of its class and—get this—is a *value* compared to similar wines. Witness Roederer Blanc de Blancs.

Roederer Blanc de Blancs is a vintage wine and is a bit more expensive than the Ruinart Champagne. I don't want to give the impression that I am portraying the two wines as competitors. But they present a good comparison in that they are quite different stylistically. In Roederer's hands, Chardonnay becomes more muscular, bold, rich, even savory. You won't be drinking this Champagne for breakfast. Whereas Ruinart minimizes its wine's contact with oxygen, Roederer vinifies one-third of the base wine in oak casks, giving its Champagne a different kind of complexity and depth from slight oxygenation (something we will explore in more detail in Chapter 4). Longer lees aging is obvious in Roederer's wine too, where the biscuit and dough flavors are in line with the wine's overall intensity. But this Champagne is not just about power. Again in contrast to Ruinart, Roederer blocks malolactic conversion. The effect is not only bracing acidity but also a more direct, pure experience of Chardonnay without obscuration. It's something you really have to experience yourself; if you taste these two wines side by side, one will seem translucent and the other transparent.

To get back to my music professor, he didn't like arriving at a friend's house for dinner to discover that his host had music on in the background, especially if it was music written by a great composer. "I'm supposed to be in conversation, but I can't help paying attention to the music." That's the thing about Louis Roederer Blanc de Blancs. You can't help but notice it.

PIERRE PÉTERS CUVÉE SPECIALE LES CHÉTILLONS

Pierre Péters is one of the most celebrated growers of Chardonnay in Champagne, and the family produces a line of *blanc de blancs* Champagnes that are exquisite, top to bottom. One of the joys of exploring any wine region is to find wines whose high quality and low price can only be explained as cosmic miscalculations. If for no reason other than the fun of it, buy the estate's entry-level Champagne—Cuvée de Réserve—pour it for friends, and watch everyone go crazy! The wine is a *blanc de blancs* that contains around 30% to 40% reserve wines from a perpetual cuvée (a blend that is continuously added to and drawn from, but never completely depleted) that the family started in 1988. What stands out is the pull of opposites: on the one hand, it is energetic, light, and zippy; yet it's layered, nutty, honeyed, and aged. And somehow, for some reason, it costs about $50, which makes absolutely no sense.

But here I want to discuss another aspect of Chardonnay through a different, higher-priced Pierre Péters Champagne. The Cuvée Speciale Les Chétillons is made from grapes grown in three plots in a single vineyard in the Grand Cru village of Le Mesnil-sur-Oger. Each plot is vinified separately and blended to make a vintage wine. What you will find in this wine is an expression of Chardonnay that is distinct from what leaps out in the Ruinart and Louis Roederer Champagnes. Les Chétillons is Chardonnay at its most racy, precise, and piquant. It's where Chardonnay gives the impression of high-toned citrus, particularly lemon. And with this comes an evident textural element that you need to experience to understand Champagne. Some will call it "chalky," and if that suits you, fine. I don't prefer the term because I think it's too specific and potentially confusing. If I had to describe what can be sensed in the wine itself, I would say it's an impalpable powder. But I think the better way to describe what happens when you drink this Champagne is from the other side, from the drinker's experience. The impression you get is something unusually fine-grained on your tongue, much finer than you would experience from any tannins in red wine. It's remarkably pleasant, and yet it's in the background and only enhances the flavors in the wine, lifting them and wrapping them in an attractive package. Texture in this Champagne is like a slight, cool breeze on a warm day. You can stop and notice it any time you want, but it's doing its job even when you don't.

Selecting a Champagne can be so situational. My favorite way to celebrate New Year's Eve is to host a very small dinner party—just one or two other couples—at my home. Everyone agrees to dress up, like people used to do regularly. The term "special occasion" fits no better than here. What's the first bottle of wine I open? That's the easiest decision of the night: Pierre Péters Cuvée Speciale Les Chétillons. It's striking, but not overpowering. And if you entered my house with a bottle of Pierre Péters Cuvée de Réserve in hand, the next easy decision would be to invite you back.

Vouette et Sorbée Blanc d'Argile

When you drink Champagne, why do you do it? I'm not sure there is a bad answer to the question, but I also think there is no single best answer either. There are, instead, many different good answers, depending on the Champagne and the circumstances. Undoubtedly, one good reason to drink Champagne is that you are eating food and want a wine that pairs well with food. As it turns out, Champagne, with its high acidity, concentration of flavors, and yes, bubbles, is an excellent match for almost every type of food. Luckily, most any Champagne will serve this purpose. Of course, not all Champagnes play the role in the same way. Some, Champagnes—Ruinart Blanc de Blancs being one of them—are lighter in body and intensity. They are better suited as aperitifs, or to match with light and salty fare. If movie theaters ever figure out that Champagnes like this are the very best partners popcorn ever met, they could just give the tickets away and still make out like bandits.

Many other Champagnes, however, don't merely pair well with food; they are experienced as incomplete without food. Like most still wines, they aren't natural soloists. You perceive a pleasant weightiness, opacity even, that is not overbearing but compels you to reach with your free hand for solid food to equilibrate the density of the wine. I know this concept is unfamiliar to some wine drinkers. I've seen many middle-aged men in dark suits leaning on food-bare restaurant bars, swirling large bowls of menacing, tannic red wines. I don't know what's really going on there or how to help them.

For everyone else, try Vouette et Sorbée Blanc d'Argile, first without food, and then with something like fried chicken. The wine is made in the south of Champagne, in the warmer subregion of the Côte des Bar. It's closer to Chablis, geographically, viticulturally, and spiritually than to the heart of the Champagne region. Here, you will find winemakers with independent streaks bordering on the rebellious, arguably a reaction to historical antipathy coming from the north. Many of my favorite wines are made in this corner of Champagne. In the case of the grower Bertrand Gautherot, proprietor of Vouette et Sorbée, you have a person who makes a *blanc de blancs* in a subregion known mostly for Pinot Noir, crops his vines to low yields in opposition to the convention in Champagne to generate high yields, ferments the wine in oak, adds no dosage, and calls it Blanc d'Argile ("white clay"). The result? A wine in the model of Grand Cru Chablis: robust, mouth-filling, perceivably influenced by oak, perhaps not quite as refreshing as other Champagnes, yet lifted by conspicuous acidity. Drinking this without food is, in comparison to a typical *blanc de blancs*, more of a meditative experience than a party in a glass, a wine for sitting instead of standing. And if you've never had Grand Cru Chablis, ask one of your best friends to bring a bottle for a nice dinner, and serve the two wines with any full-flavored chicken dish. You won't need popcorn.

LILBERT-FIS BLANC DE BLANCS BRUT

If, at the moment, you don't want your wine to be serious, and you don't want to meditate over your wine, and you aren't interested in investigating food and wine pairings, then may I introduce you to good old-fashioned uncomplicated hedonism? How about hedonism for around $50?

The idea that pleasure is the highest value in Champagne is widespread, but various competing beliefs appear to be ascending. For the most part, I think that's fine. But some trends give me pause. There's a confounding contemporary notion that what matters primarily is not the experience of *drinking* a Champagne, but is instead the *method* of making Champagne in conformity with the zeitgeist that calls for less human intervention and fewer additives, particularly dosage and sulfur. Some wines made this way turn out to be wonderful. Others can be very austere or muted. The twisted logic used to prop up the Champagnes that are not delicious is that if a drinker experiences the wine as less hedonic than last year's version, that's actually confirmation of the winemaker's rigor. If this is your thing, great. Personally, I drink wine, in part, for relief from the grim and the dull.

Thankfully, relief is abundant in Champagne. Lilbert's entry-level *blanc de blancs* is fun, voluptuous, supple, old-school Champagne. It's creamy and doughy. It's an example of Chardonnay's flavors leaning slightly to the brash side: orange instead of lemon; pear rather than apple. It's not sweet, but it's not unsweetened. And it's graceful and balanced too, with fragrant fruit and brioche sitting atop pleasant salinity and signature acidity. That's what is so great about a Champagne like this: it's delicious but not simple. The main difference between this wine and the other *blanc de blancs* we've looked at so far is not qualitative; it's that this Champagne makes you want to laugh, gulp it, spill it, pour more, open more, and not give a damn. It's as if Lilbert designed this Champagne for conviviality. If you could be transported back to 1963 to hang out with Dean Martin at the Sands Hotel, this is a Champagne you'd want to bring along for the ride.

As for the Lilbert family, it has grown vines in Champagne for 300 years and has been making relatively small quantities of wine for the last hundred. I have no idea if the family has a theory about wine, but if I had to guess, I'd say the theory has more to do with joy than process. For myself, I'll crack open the joy and be grateful.

TAITTINGER COMTES DE CHAMPAGNE BLANC DE BLANCS

I can't think of a better place to end this exploration of Chardonnay than with one of the most classic, renowned vintage *blanc de blancs* in Champagne. Taittinger Comtes de Champagne brings us back to the beginning of this section, but it makes more sense when you've already tried other *blanc de blancs* first. I said that Chardonnay is the perfect Champagne grape variety in part because its subtle flavors complement the flavors of autolysis, and I pointed to Ruinart Blanc de Blancs as an exemplar. Comtes de Champagne demonstrates how this proposition is expressed by a different producer, at a higher level of quality, and in a vintage wine. Like Ruinart's wine, Comtes de Champagne is fermented in stainless steel and undergoes malolactic conversion, although one difference is that a small percentage of the base wine is aged for a short time in barrels. But the two main differences are that Comtes de Champagne is made from more highly selected wines from grapes grown in superior Champagne vineyards in a single year, and that Comtes de Champagne undergoes long lees aging for six to ten years. Now the trick is to produce a wine whose elements do not stand out and clash, like two superstars on a basketball team who each could rack up individual statistics every night, but who instead harmonize such that you notice a great team as something apart from its members. In Comtes de Champagne, Chardonnay is a star that expresses substantial fruit character, but not in the way that overtly fruity wines do. The brilliance in this wine is that Chardonnay's flavors stand up to, complement, and marry with, the prominent toasted and baked bread flavors to create a Champagne that is not loud, but moving.

Taittinger Comtes de Champagne is what is known in Champagne as a prestige cuvée. Large Champagne houses, and some smaller ones, often organize their offerings by style and quality, though they don't all do so in the same ways. *Blanc de blancs* is an example of a style; other styles include vintage and non-vintage Champagnes, *blanc de noirs*, rosé Champagnes, and Champagnes of various sweetness levels. These style categories can overlap. For example, Taittinger produces three different rosé Champagnes, one of which is a vintage wine, and one of which is sweeter than the others. In terms of quality, a house's least expensive Champagne usually will be a non-vintage wine, made from grapes that are not the very best the house can access, and aged a shorter amount of time than the house's most expensive wines. I say "usually" because exceptions abound; for example, Krug does not produce an inexpensive wine. At the high end—again, usually—you will find a house's prestige cuvée. Well-known examples are Dom Pérignon and Cristal. It might be better to say prestige cuvées, plural, because often—as is the case with Dom Pérignon, Cristal, and Comtes de Champagne—the house produces both a white and a rosé prestige cuvée with the same brand name. A prestige cuvée is a Champagne house's way of saying, "We'll show you what our house can do when we put our best foot forward, though you will need to pay for the privilege."

We should expect—demand—much from Comtes de Champagne. One important quality you look for in a great wine is length—the longer the pleasant flavors of the wine persist harmoniously in your mouth after you have swallowed, teasing your brain, the better. And then there is a wine like Comtes de Champagne. It delivers physical length and something else. Long after the sensation of taste is gone, the next day, when you are taking a walk alone, a vivid memory of the smell and taste of the wine arises out of nowhere, and you smile. That's when you know, in a very personal way, the promise and the joy of *blanc de blancs* Champagne.

Pinot Noir

Black grapes such as Pinot Noir are used to make red wine, as every drinker knows. Sparkling Shiraz and Lambrusco perhaps are the most notable examples of red wines turned sparkling. But under French law, Champagne cannot be red. Champagne production is almost all white, save for about 10% of rosé Champagne. Yet, two black grapes—Pinot Noir and Pinot Meunier—account for 70% of Champagne's grapevine plantings. Not only is Pinot Noir the most commonly grown grape variety in Champagne, there is more Pinot Noir planted in Champagne than in any other wine region in the world.

What is going on here? Why go to the trouble of extracting clear juice from black grapes, making the effort to avoid coloration that normally occurs when grape juice interacts with broken grape skins? Why not just grow white grapes to produce white sparkling wines?

In part, the answer is historical and practical. Pinot Noir was grown in Champagne and made into still wine for hundreds of years before the Champenois began producing sparkling wines. The grape was there, as was Pinot Meunier, when Champagne became a sparkling wine.

Sometimes the answer to why we used anything for some purpose was that it was within arm's reach. Sometimes we just use what we have and hope for the best.

As it turns out, though, Pinot Noir is a fantastic partner with a white grape—in this case, Chardonnay—in sparkling wine blends. There are some practical reasons: compared to other black grapes, Pinot Noir has a low level of anthocyanins (the pigments in black grapes that are responsible for the color of red wine), making it easier to press juice without coloration. Like Chardonnay, Pinot Noir ripens early, retaining acidity (though not as much as Chardonnay) in Champagne's cold climate while achieving flavor ripeness. Pinot Noir and Chardonnay respond differently to various diseases, which means that in a year when one suffers, the other might thrive, giving producers more flexibility to make sufficient quantities of wine. But the two contributions Pinot Noir makes to Champagne blends that matter most to drinkers are flavor and texture.

As I have emphasized, the flavors that Chardonnay brings to Champagne are subtle and complement the flavors of autolysis. Other white grapes that can grow in Champagne's cold environment don't do what Chardonnay does, nor can they bring anything else to the table that would improve a Champagne blend (in some cases, quite the opposite). Pinot Noir's aromas and flavors are varied, complementary, and, crucially, relatively understated. Pinot Noir commonly is associated with aromas in wine such as roses, red fruits (for example, cherries and strawberries), spices (cinnamon, cloves), and savory elements such as mushrooms. You often will find these aromas in Pinot Noir in Champagne. But at Champagne's high latitude, and when pressed off of its skins and put through a second fermentation and autolysis, Pinot Noir can spin off aromas we don't usually associate with still wines made from this grape: apricots, apples, golden raisins, orange marmalade, and other aromas, that are not, for the lack of a better term, dark. The range of aromas and flavors in Pinot Noir add complexity to Champagne blends with Chardonnay without depriving Champagne of its characteristic elegance and restraint.

The second important contribution made by Pinot Noir in Champagne is that it affects a wine's texture—as I mentioned earlier, the way a sip of Champagne feels in your mouth, apart from how it smells or tastes. Some writers and winemakers will say that Pinot Noir *adds* body, structure, or "backbone" to Champagne, but these statements are somewhat misleading. Champagnes made 100% from Chardonnay do not lack body, structure, or "backbone" (to the extent that term has meaning in wine). Pinot Noir may contribute certain textural elements to a Champagne blend, but the more important matter—again, we are talking about blends, not components welded together—is that Pinot Noir *influences* the overall texture of a wine. In Champagne, Pinot Noir typically is experienced in the mouth as softer, rounder, and silkier; less acidic, steely, crisp, or sharp than Chardonnay. When purely textural components are experienced in combination with Pinot Noir's aromas and flavors, Pinot Noir can seem, metaphorically, warmer than Chardonnay. It's the merger of different textural elements from Chardonnay and Pinot Noir that contribute to a harmonious complexity, which is a hallmark of great wine.

Of course, a good way to start the process of understanding what a single part contributes to the whole is to examine the part itself, and we can do this by drinking Champagnes made 100% from Pinot Noir. These wines are much less common than *blanc de blancs. Blanc de noirs* ("white of blacks") is a term used to describe a white Champagne made exclusively from black grapes. Most are made entirely from Pinot Noir, a much small number are composed entirely of Pinot Meunier, and an even smaller number are a blend of both grapes. I enjoy these wines very much, but I suspect that the reason they are produced in relatively small quantities is that they aren't what most consumers expect from

Champagne. But putting preferences aside, these wines are interesting and instructive. Let's try three *blanc de noirs* made entirely from Pinot Noir.

ULYSSE COLLIN LES MAILLONS BLANC DE NOIRS EXTRA BRUT

Wine exists to be drunk by a drinker. This truth is easily forgotten in lavish profiles of winemakers and their philosophies and interests: without drinkers and *their* interests, there would be little wine. No matter how intellectually or morally compelling a winemaker or winemaker's technique may be, a wine that does not deliver something—anything— captivating in the glass, is a wine with no great purpose. Champagne drinkers expect and deserve something more than mere refreshment for their money—and it is their money that is exchanged. It seems to me that if we want to single out an individual winemaker for praise, we should do so from the perspective of the consumer: what is the drinker getting from the trade?

Olivier Collin is a master of Champagne who takes risks that would cause lesser winemakers to fall on their faces, and the rewards are reaped by the drinker. He makes Champagne in ways that are about as natural and non-interventionist as one can get: for example, fermentation is carried out with indigenous yeasts (almost all Champagne is made by inoculating grape must with specially selected yeasts that are known to be especially suitable for Champagne); fermentation and storage is in used barrels; the wines are not fined or filtered. In combination with the fact that in the Les Maillons vineyard Pinot Noir is grown to a high degree of ripeness, the result is a wine that presents Pinot Noir unobstructed. This wine is a delicious window into the two key elements discussed above: aromas and texture.

In this *blanc de noirs*, Pinot Noir's aromas and flavors are what you would expect from red Burgundy: it's floral and spicy, with delicate red fruit with a savory edge. What is remarkable is how crystalline the wine is in this respect; Pinot Noir is not hidden, transformed, or lost in the shuffle of winemaking. There are pastry and brioche aromas from autolysis as well as light dosage, which make the overall aroma profile undeniably Champagne. It's Pinot Noir wearing its tuxedo.

The texture is notable too. Champagne's mouthfeel should always be marked by bubbles and high acidity. Without both, something is wrong. But high acidity doesn't always mean the highest possible acidity. In this wine, Pinot Noir doesn't deliver the searing acidity found in some *blanc de blancs*. The acidity is high enough to lift the wine and make it refreshing, but the overall impression compared to most *blanc de blancs* is perceptibly more supple, more mouthcoating, more viscous. The term "vinous" sometimes is used for Champagnes like this one. It's an odd usage because vinous means "resembling wine," and sparkling wines are, in fact, wines. But the idea is that certain sparkling wines call to mind the textural sensations normally associated with still wines, even though the bubbles are a prominent feature. With this wine, you can experience directly what Pinot Noir can do to the texture of Champagne.

Oh, and the wine is absolutely delicious. I'm guessing that Olivier Collin doesn't produce Ulysse Collin Les Maillons Blanc de Noirs to show off winemaking techniques or to demonstrate the characteristics of Pinot Noir in Champagne. He makes it for drinkers to drink it. So, go ahead and analyze, understand, and remember—and then enjoy.

Egly-Ouriet Blanc de Noirs Les Crayères

In Chapter 1, I mentioned a wine I will not be discussing in this book because of its outrageous price—Krug Clos d'Ambonnay. But I will say this: Krug is one of the greatest Champagne houses, and it chose a walled vineyard in Ambonnay for its signature *blanc de noirs* for good reason. If you want to experience Pinot Noir that is quintessentially Champagne, you will be hard pressed to find wines from a village better suited for the job than Ambonnay. That's because Pinot Noir from

Ambonnay tends to be much like Champagne itself: characterful but refined; familiar but complex; energetic but graceful. Of course, that does not mean that Champagnes made from Pinot Noir in Ambonnay are all the same, which brings us to the next two wines.

Egly-Ouriet is perhaps the most well-known producer in Ambonnay, and Francis Egly has managed to generate cultish attention to his wines (as reflected in the prices). Pinot Noir is harvested from old vines at full ripeness, resulting in a very concentrated wine. But the aromas and flavors in this *blanc de noirs* are different from those in the Ulysse Collin wine. In this Champagne, Pinot Noir's flavor profile is not dominated by red fruits but brings in golden favors of apricots, yellow raisins, honey, caramel, and hazelnuts, combined with pie dough and smoke from long lees aging. The texture is about as viscous as you'll experience in Champagne, not in the way of a dense still wine or a luscious sweet wine, but nevertheless giving the sense that you don't so much drink this wine as lap it up. It's a thrilling, intense experience; a rich, long wine. Here again, importantly, the wine's crisp acidity—while not nearly as significant as in Chardonnay-dominated Champagnes—is the key to holding everything together.

This points to a somewhat perplexing and, ultimately, redeeming quality about great bottles of Champagne. Great Champagne doesn't walk you down any single, well-marked path. It doesn't always look like the same object when viewed from different angles. Here we have a wine that, in some sense, is like a pleasant dose of a narcotic: everything it draws into your senses is richer, brighter, creamier, more colorful than normal. If that's all it did, well, that might be good enough. But what sets this Champagne apart is that the underlying elements whose volumes are being turned up to eleven are themselves soft, light, and mellow. It's in this way that Egly-Ouriet Blanc de Noirs Les Crayères demonstrates so well the range of what Pinot Noir in Champagne can be and can do.

PAUL DÉTHUNE BLANC DE NOIRS BRUT

Paul Déthune is another outstanding grower in Ambonnay, producing high-quality wines that lack only the cachet of Egly-Ouriet's. Like Egly-Ouriet, Paul Déthune makes a single-vineyard *blanc de noirs* from Les Crayeres (at about half the price). But I'm going to discuss its basic Ambonnay *blanc de noirs* instead, to offer a point.

If it's correct to assume that price matters to consumers, it's interesting to investigate what the differences are, if any, between the high-end, single-vineyard Champagne of a revered producer like Egly-Ouriet and the basic, village-level (albeit Grand Cru village) Champagne of a merely excellent producer like Paul Déthune. One wine costs more than three times the price of the other. I invite you to discover the differences for yourself. But I will tell you some of my thoughts. First, these wines inarguably are comparable, in that they express Ambonnay Pinot Noir in very similar ways. The aromas and flavors are not identical, but they are more similar than they are different. Line up these wines with a Champagne from outside Ambonnay, and these two will be more alike than the third. There is a meaningful stylistic difference between the wines, which I will discuss below, but when you put that aside, what are the qualitative differences? You might find one or more, or believe you have, if you look; but here's the point: there is no qualitative difference that accounts for the extraordinary price disparity, and Paul Déthune Blanc de Noirs is a model of Pinot Noir pleasure in Ambonnay. You don't have to spend a fortune to drink wonderful Champagne. All you really have to do is be curious, explore with an open mind, and be honest with yourself about what you notice.

Now, as to the stylistic difference. I've mentioned ripe grapes in praise of Champagnes made from them, and it's easy to get caught up in the idea that riper is necessarily better. This is not true. Grapes are ripe in a window of time, not at a precise moment. Whether grapes should be harvested today or tomorrow (or should have been harvested yesterday or the day before) often is a matter of legitimate differences of opinion or, in many cases, a difference of style. Pierre and Sophie Déthune prefer to harvest grapes in Ambonnay earlier than some of their neighbors—not early, but not late. The grapes are ripe, but the Champagnes made from them exhibit freshness and restraint that arguably is more in line with traditional Champagne. That's obvious from this wine. On the one hand, it has all of the warmth, texture, and flavors you would want from Pinot Noir; I've enjoyed this wine with a steak, for goodness' sake. But the volume on the wine is turned down to a modest level, a comfortable level. Is louder music better? Is more fruit concentration in wine better? I don't think so, necessarily. There are Champagnes that show what can be accomplished, and there are wines that reveal what is fundamental, classic, timeless. Paul Déthune Blanc de Noirs is this second type of Champagne.

Pinot Meunier

I've wondered at times what it must be like to have an extraordinarily famous, successful older sibling. What if your big brother ends up being the President of the United States, or the best quarterback in the NFL and headed for the Hall of Fame, or the founder and CEO of the world's largest company and a generous philanthropist? Whatever success you may have, however virtuous a person you may be, one thing everyone will know for sure about you is that *you are not the other guy*. That's what it's like to be Pinot Meunier.

The relationship between Pinot Noir and Pinot Meunier is quite close. In fact, although it's common to speak of Pinot Noir and Pinot Meunier as different grape varieties, they actually are merely different mutations of a single grape variety, Pinot. Pinot Noir is the oldest known Pinot mutation, is world famous, and is considered one of the greatest wine grapes on the planet. Elite Burgundy producers can ferment Pinot Noir into wines that retail for over $10,000 a bottle. Meanwhile, Pinot

Meunier is rarely grown outside Champagne. In Champagne, Pinot Meunier has been treated like the class clown who, though fun and exciting in small doses, is thought to be a lightweight otherwise. The smart, sophisticated kids are either too snobbish to hang out with him or too embarrassed to admit that they do. While it's easy to find people in Champagne who will wax ecstatically about the grandness of Chardonnay and Pinot Noir, Pinot Meunier—if discussed at all—most commonly is described as merely bringing "fruitiness" or perhaps "softness" to the blend, while it also is derided for supposedly not being age-worthy.

Why, then, is Pinot Meunier the second-most grown grape in Champagne, ahead of Chardonnay? One answer you might hear is, essentially, that Pinot Meunier assists in the production of easy-drinking, chug-it-right-away Champagnes that appeal to the majority of consumers who have no intention of holding on to their wines for very long (which is good, because if they did, the Pinot Meunier supposedly would fall apart and ruin the wine). It's an interesting theory that permits a role for Pinot Meunier while also justifying being snobbish about it. But I don't think this narrative accurately captures what is going on. Let's look at a few facts.

Pinot Meunier is—not surprisingly—fairly similar to Pinot Noir. Not the same, but similar. If you drink a good glass of still Pinot Meunier from the Champagne region, you will notice that it smells and tastes much more like Pinot Noir than any other black grape variety. Thus, a producer who blends Pinot Meunier into a Champagne produces a sparkling wine that a drinker will easily recognize as Champagne, not some other sparkling wine from another wine region. This is beneficial for Champagne producers for at least two reasons.

First, as mentioned earlier, inexpensive Champagne is in high demand in some European markets. Pinot Meunier is, on average, less expensive for producers to acquire than Chardonnay or Pinot Noir, and it makes more economic sense to use a higher proportion of Pinot

Meunier in these wines. Second, because Pinot Meunier develops buds on its vines later than Pinot Noir but ripens earlier, it is more likely to survive through harvest in years when weather and disease pressures, such as spring frosts and late-season rain, are particularly challenging. Put simply, Pinot Meunier is hardier and more reliable than Pinot Noir (and Chardonnay, for that matter), and producers may need significant quantities of it in any particular year to make enough wine.

None of this suggests that Pinot Meunier is a markedly inferior grape, that it cannot produce complex wines, or that it does not age well. And there really is no convincing evidence for these judgments. To the contrary, in the 21st century, a number of skilled growers have demonstrated that Champagnes made entirely from Pinot Meunier can be outstanding; some of these wines have achieved cult status and high price-points. Among the large houses, Krug makes liberal use of Pinot Meunier in its highly rated and age-worthy wines. To take one example, Krug's 2002 vintage Champagne, which currently retails at around $400-500 a bottle, contains 21% Pinot Meunier. I'll let you guess whether all of that Pinot Meunier has killed the wine's vibe after twenty years. What is true is that Pinot Meunier's reputation has never approached those of Pinot Noir or Chardonnay. And I suppose being third in a group of three puts you in last place, if that matters to anyone.

The purpose of my defense of Pinot Meunier is merely to encourage you, once again, to investigate wines for yourself without getting too seduced by the preferences of others, including biases about Pinot Meunier. Pinot Meunier can bring an elevated level of bright, fresh fruit and floral notes to some blends. It also can deliver interesting dried-fruit and savory aromas. Pinot Meunier has high acidity, which, as we know, is critical in Champagne. But find out for yourself. When we get to the blends, I will suggest wines that have significant proportions of Pinot Meunier and others that have none. As I have said, the art of blending in Champagne is about making—in a certain style, for a particular market—a whole wine that is experienced not as a number of parts but as a composite. Two wines that share the same percentage of Pinot Meunier can be significantly different because of the multitude of different winemaking choices available to producers.

Blanc de noirs made from Pinot Meunier represent a tiny slice of total Champagne production. Fortunately, within that slice are a growing number of remarkable wines made by some of the best growers and smaller producers in Champagne. Each of the following three wines is a testament to the potential of Pinot Meunier.

Moussé Fils Special Club

Champagne labels are not always models of clarity, often bearing various terms and descriptions that may or may not have legal or technical meanings and, even when they do, are not necessarily informative for the average consumer. For example, the term *vieilles vignes* ("old vines") suggests something vaguely positive, but it is unregulated and has no legal meaning. And then there is the term "Special Club," which is generally descriptive, even if you don't know precisely what it means. The Club Trésors de Champagne is an invitation-only organization of fewer than thirty quality grape growers who produce Champagne. As is the case with any self-respecting club, gaining admission is just the beginning of the test. In vintage years that the members decide are outstanding, each producer may submit one vintage wine for the club's consideration, which involves blind tastings after the first fermentation and after three years of aging. Wines that are deemed worthy (not all are) may be sold in the club's unique bottle and may be labeled "Special Club." In 2005, the club for the first time gave its stamp of approval to a Champagne made entirely of Pinot Meunier. That wine, made by Moussé Fils, has continued to be certified by the club in the years since. It's fitting, because this wine is a perfect example of Pinot Meunier showing its colors in peacock fashion.

Moussé Fils is a small house in a small village dominated by Pinot Meunier. The Moussé family bottles several wines that consist mostly of Pinot Meunier, but it's the 100% Pinot Meunier Special Club that shows that this grape variety can easily stand on its own. In the 2014 bottling, it's fruity, for sure, but the fruit profile is complex: you might sense cherries, oranges, apricots, and even tropical fruit. Secondarily, the wine is nutty and spicy. This broad array of aromas and flavors is a prime indication of a wine that cannot be described as simple. Texturally, this wine is rich, opulent, and full-bodied, without being overbearing or heavy. And it's long. This is a hedonic wine, but it's distinctively Champagne, structured by acidity and soft bubbles.

This is what Pinot Meunier can offer in the right hands. Is it special? Yes. However, it's no longer unique. Moussé Fils was the first member of the Club Trésors de Champagne to win approval for a 100% Pinot Meunier *blanc de noirs*, but it was not the last. And if the success of this Champagne is any indication, there will be more to come.

BÉRÊCHE ET FILS RIVE GAUCHE

One of my favorite Champagne producers is a family estate operated by two brothers, Raphaël and Vincent Bérêche. Bérêche does not focus solely on Pinot Meunier but, instead, makes a range of wines from all three grape varieties and from vineyards in different areas of Champagne. Bérêche consistently makes complex, fascinating wines that are notable for their refinement and elegance. These aren't among Champagne's most expensive wines, but, in a sense, they seem that they *must* be—like you paid for a small hotel room but somehow opened the door to a two-story suite. These are wines you feel uncomfortable opening when you're wearing casual clothes. You think, *I should be eating lobster at a fine restaurant with a view in Chamonix Mont Blanc.* Or something like that. This might be easy to accept by now, if we are talking about Pinot Noir or Chardonnay. But Pinot Meunier? Yes. Pinot Meunier too.

Like Moussé Special Club, Rive Gauche is produced from vines planted in a vineyard in the Vallée de la Marne, though a few miles to the south on the left bank of the Marne ("Rive Gauche" means "left bank"). But while Moussé's wine is fermented in stainless steel and undergoes malolactic conversion, Rive Gauche is vinified in barrel, and malolactic conversion is blocked. As we have seen in other examples, these choices can be meaningful. Texturally, Rive Gauche is much fresher, with higher acidity and greater liveliness. Pinot Meunier in this Champagne shows its slimmer side, a side that leans less on overt ripeness in fruit and more on purity. The fruit is toned down, but it comes across as crisper, more defined. The herbal, smoky, savory sides of Pinot Meunier arrive in whispers, in harmony with the fruit. This is a Champagne that is very flavorful but not overrun with flavor.

Bérêche Rive Gauche is Pinot Meunier showing that it is not the class clown all day long, and right now it's wearing a suit and tie. The dismissive labels "fruity" and "soft" and other pejoratives typically lobbed at Pinot Meunier do not apply easily. Nor can I think of a good reason why a wine with this structure and flavor profile would disintegrate if you held on to it for a few years to see what might happen after some bottle age. I will say this: if you don't drink this wine with food, then drink it alone or with someone else who can appreciate it. And who is well dressed.

Chartogne-Taillet Les Barres

Alexandre Chartogne-Taillet is another highly talented and dedicated grower-producer in Champagne, a further testament to the fact that, as I've said, we are living in a golden age of Champagne. Like Bérêche, Chartogne-Taillet carefully makes a range of well-appreciated wines from all three grape varieties. What Chartogne-Taillet has done with his single-vineyard Les Barres *blanc de noirs* is to give us yet another reason to appreciate Pinot Meunier.

Somewhere between the fruity richness of Moussé Special Club and the arresting elegance of Bérêche Rive Gauche sits a Goldilocks wine from a different subregion than the first two, the Montagne de Reims. There are delicious wines. And there are fascinating wines. Great wines are, to one extent or another, both delicious and fascinating. And then there are wines like Chartogne-Taillet Les Barres that are delicious, and fascinating, and make you laugh for some reason you can't explain, except that you've been gently pushed off your balance and think it's funny.

Les Barres is, on the one hand, the full Pinot Meunier *blanc de noirs* fireworks show: fruity, floral, round and full-bodied, herbal, smoky, and toasty. The overall profile is harmonious, so that you really can't say that it tilts toward or away from fruitiness or any other description. It's something in between the first two wines. But there also is an underlying sense of salinity to it, an element that gives the Champagne an unexpected twist of complexity, texture, and flavor. That's what is so wonderful about this Champagne; it has everything you find in the best of Pinot Meunier, and instead of going left or right, it digs down deeper to deliver an experience of Pinot Meunier that is both familiar and unfamiliar.

Pinot Meunier, it should be admitted, has much greater range, much greater potential, more gravitas than historically believed. No, it will never be Pinot Noir. But who cares, really? To be consumed solely with the question of what in Champagne is best or better, or with reputations and history, is to leave a ton of joy on the table. In Champagne, Pinot Meunier is different, interesting, and, in some cases, fascinating and delicious. That should be well enough to justify the exploration.

Blends of Black and White Grapes

As we have seen, Chardonnay, Pinot Noir, and Pinot Meunier each have the capacity to make diverse, expressive, and wonderful Champagnes.

But the vast majority of white Champagnes are blends of at least two of these grapes, and most commonly all three. This makes sense because Chardonnay, Pinot Noir, and Pinot Meunier each are able to bring different structural and flavor elements to a blend, resulting in balanced wines that are distinctively Champagne. The best-selling and perhaps most famous Champagne, Moët & Chandon Brut Impérial, is toasty, fresh, with subdued fruit; it's exactly what most people expect Champagne to be. And it's a blend of the three grapes in roughly equal proportions. Champagne blends of Chardonnay, Pinot Noir, and Pinot Meunier are some of the most expensive and some of the cheapest Champagnes; they can be great wines and uninspiring wines; wines that make you happy to be alive and wines that make you wonder what the hell happened. Perhaps more importantly, blends of the three grape varieties come in all manner of formulations and proportions, presenting drinkers with vast opportunities to delve into differences in styles.

It's this diversity within the category of blends that, sadly, is lost on so many consumers who enjoy Champagne but for whom "Champagne is Champagne"—where significant differences are expected only along a price continuum. The dominant purpose of this book is to nudge more Champagne drinkers to get themselves out of that mindset and appreciate the kaleidoscope of wines in Champagne. Even just focusing on different types of grape blends, I can't do more in this book than get you started, given the multitude of very different Champagnes. But with the next six wines, we can at least begin to see what can happen when Chardonnay, Pinot Noir, and Pinot Meunier come together.

POL ROGER BRUT RÉSERVE

Known as "White Foil" (because, of course, the foil is white), the brut non-vintage wine produced by the esteemed house of Pol Roger is unusual in that it is made of equal parts Chardonnay, Pinot Noir, and

Pinot Meunier. White Foil is a very good Champagne, especially at its price point. And it gives us the opportunity to see what happens when a high-quality producer makes a Champagne that doesn't lean on any one of the three varieties.

White Foil is a great example of a Champagne that is both attractive and harmonious. It's not bland or boring; it has plenty of character—it's floral, fruity, bready, creamy, spicy, piquant. It has bright acidity and a soft mousse. If you pay attention, you can break down the wine and glimpse the various influences of Chardonnay, Pinot Noir, and Pinot Meunier at work. But when you take in this Champagne as a whole—in other words, when you drink it—no aroma or flavor, or categories of aromas or flavors, or grape varieties, predominate. No textural components stick out like a sore thumb. They work together seamlessly in a fresh, energetic, people-pleasing Champagne. It's hard to imagine that very many drinkers would dislike White Foil, which throws a fastball right down the middle of the Champagne strike zone.

Of course, any product that is excellent and yet not particularly distinctive risks being lost in a marketplace filled with similar items. In Champagne, as elsewhere, producers have a solution that undoubtedly affects the drinking experience: branding and marketing. Champagne houses spend enormous sums of money to promote their brands to consumers and separate them from competitors on crowded shelves. It's interesting to observe that wine producers usually try to sell you on who they are: their families, history, traditions, craftsmanship, techniques. You are told where they live, how many horses they have, what philosophies they accept and those they doubt, what they care about and what they hope to achieve. You, the consumer, are supposed to buy wine to connect with *them*. Spirits companies usually do the exact opposite: they sell you products based on who *you* are or would like to be. If you drink a particular spirit, you are sophisticated, or carefree, or mature, or young, or conservative, or unconventional. Visit Absolut's website and see how long it takes to figure out who you are if you drink that brand of vodka.

Champagne producers seem to ride in both lanes at times, drawing you into the story of the house and making you a player in it. It's worth paying attention to who is telling you what about a particular Champagne, and how. Nobody is immune to the effects of marketing, promotion, packaging, socialization, culture, and journalism on how we perceive a wine when we drink it. We don't buy or drink Champagne blind, outside of an artificial exercise. Just as it makes little sense to speak of Coke as merely a sugary, flavored carbonated beverage, it's not possible to understand what Champagne is without considering the stories we are told about Champagne or Champagne brands and the stories we tell ourselves.

But sometimes, standing back and observing can grant us a little freedom. Take Pol Roger. For whatever reason, Pol Roger appears intent on capturing the stodgy, old-fashioned, cigar-chomping set. Visit Pol Roger's website, and you'll find images of dark wood and leather chairs, multiple references to the fact that Pol Roger was Winston Churchill's favorite Champagne, and the statement—not exceptionally consistent with modern cultural norms—that "Pol Roger is the gentlemen's Champagne." It must be working to some extent, because you can find serious commentators referring to Pol Roger Champagne as "masculine." Maybe I just haven't looked hard enough, but I don't detect masculinity or femininity or anything in between in White Foil. And while I am a fan of Pol Roger's entire line of Champagnes, I like to think that my appreciation of them has nothing to do with whether, or whenever, I am a gentleman. White Foil is, as I've said, the kind of Champagne that should be universally appealing to drinkers; for the person who appreciates Champagne for what it offers in the glass, what else does it really need to be?

VEUVE CLICQUOT BRUT

Now let's tilt to one side and take a look at what happens when Pinot Noir is the dominant grape in a blend. Veuve Clicquot is known for its work with Pinot Noir, which is the primary component in all of its blends. Its ubiquitous "Yellow Label" (named for—well, you know) is composed of 50% to 55% Pinot Noir, 28% to 33% Chardonnay, and 15% to 20% Pinot Meunier. There is a lot going on with this wine, but notice what predominates. The most salient aromas are dark or red: roses, apples, cherries, strawberries. The yeasty aromas are dark and spicy, too: rye instead of sourdough. And the texture is rich, substantial, and mouthcoating. These are all hallmarks of Pinot Noir.

But they are just tips in one direction. Yellow Label is more autumn than spring, more dusk than dawn. Drinking Yellow Label triggers a desire for a meal to pair with it, whether you're hungry or not. Here, too, we see excellence in the craft of blending. The wine is driven by Pinot Noir, but Chardonnay and Pinot Meunier—all in the right proportions—ensure balance. Yellow Label is full-bodied, but it is not heavy. In particular, Chardonnay makes the wine vivacious, with acidity that is not bracing but refreshing. Pinot Meunier brightens the fruit profile without changing the wine's overall focus. Yellow Label is popular for good reason, and, if anything, it is an underappreciated Champagne.

Which brings me to another aspect of Champagne weirdness. Sometimes a little awareness of brand associations is counterproductive. Yellow Label is one of the most prevalent Champagnes in restaurants. If an American restaurant offers any Champagne at all (and I mean Champagne, not sparkling wine), the chances are that Yellow Label is on the menu. Somehow, that seems to be a strike against it for those who have stretched their Champagne legs and can rattle off the names of today's most popular growers. It's as if a natural evolution of Champagne drinking is to grow out of Yellow Label and look upon it as the Champagne of the unsophisticated. How strange and unnecessary. Pour this wine in a glass and take some time with it, away from anyone too cool for school. Taste the wine, not the label or any associations with the label. I think you'll be hard pressed to dispute that Yellow Label is a superb expression of a Pinot Noir-dominant blend at a fair price. And luckily, you can have it any time you go out.

Laurent-Perrier La Cuvée

Like any other industry that succeeds in the long term, the Champagne business is not static. Consumer trends and other market forces push growers and producers in various directions. And one thing consumers appear to want more of today in their Champagne is Chardonnay. One manifestation of the Chardonnay trend is Laurent-Perrier's decision a few years ago to modify the blend of its basic blend (which already was Chardonnay-dominant) to add a higher percentage of Chardonnay. La Cuvée is an excellent example of a wine that leans in the opposite way of Yellow Label, with 55% Chardonnay, 30% to 35% Pinot Noir, and 10% to 15% Pinot Meunier.

To be clear, we can't make a precise comparison between La Cuvée and Yellow Label. The wines are made by two different producers and built somewhat differently, putting aside the grape-variety compositions. To take one example, Yellow Label includes more and older reserve wines than does La Cuvée, which in part explains why La Cuvée is experienced as fresher and younger. But if you put these two wines side by side, there is no doubt that one is powered by Pinot Noir and the other by Chardonnay. The initial aromas of La Cuvée are much closer to those of Ruinart's *blanc de blancs* than to those of Yellow Label. La Cuvée is light and airy, with aromas and flavors associated with Chardonnay, such as green apples and citrus. The autolytic notes tend toward lightly toasted white bread. The acidity is crisp, racy. All signs point to Chardonnay. But once again, that's not the whole story, because the smaller portions of Pinot Noir and Pinot Meunier round out the wine with their contributions of fruit and texture.

When evaluating a wine, we naturally tend to focus on what the wine *is*. What can we find in the wine? I like to think also about what a wine *does*. What do I want to do as a result of drinking this wine? As with Yellow Label, most Pinot-focused Champagne blends make me want to eat something, usually something substantial, usually featuring beef. But when I drink a Chardonnay-dominant blend like La Cuvée, fermented in stainless steel and released fairly young, I don't want food. What I really want is good company, someone who wants to talk. Aperitif wines don't stimulate appetites, as a dictionary may claim. They stimulate conversation. That's what Laurent-Perrier La Cuvée does, to me.

Françoise Bedel Dis, "Vin Secret"

The market is awash in non-vintage Champagne blends from the large and prestigious houses; in blends of the three grape varieties in roughly equal proportions or a bit more or less of one grape or another; in blends engineered to satisfy this or that house style or market demand. What the market is not awash in is a blend consisting of up to 90% Pinot Meunier, with as little as 5% Pinot Noir and 5% Chardonnay, produced by a woman who grows grapes and makes wine biodynamically—the lunar calendar determines racking and bottling dates—at the very western (and unfashionable) edge of Champagne. Yes, this Champagne is unusual in how it is made. But I think it's worth pausing to consider a couple of points.

In the first place, it demonstrates the point that excellent blends can have more than small skews toward one grape variety or another. In this case, Pinot Meunier isn't just driving the blend; it owns the blend, with what amounts to seasoning from the two other varieties. It's a heady wine that definitely is about Pinot Meunier, with its vivid red fruit and floral aromas, mouthcoating texture, and distinct savoriness.

What exactly are the small amounts of Chardonnay and Pinot Noir doing in there? I honestly don't know. I just know that this works, that all the components are in consonance, that whatever led Françoise and her son Vincent to decide on the blend—whether it be the moon or what—they did a great job. Ultimately, percentages of grape varieties' contributions are interesting and, many times, telling; but you drink the Champagne, not the math. You cannot fully accept wine without accommodating mystery.

The other issue this Champagne calls to mind—one that I address in more depth in the next chapter—is that there is no chance a large Champagne house would ever make this wine. There is a market for it, obviously, but it's a very small market. The large houses need to make Champagnes in significant volumes that please much larger consumer segments. Of course, that does not mean that grower wines are better or more praiseworthy. What it does mean is that someone like Françoise Bedel can be nimbler, can follow her heart, can experiment, and is generally free to do her own thing as long as she has some fans who will buy her wines. It's easy to get tunnel vision and to see Champagne blends as a category that consists of a small number of styles, which the various houses tweak a bit in an attempt to carve out niches. But for the curious drinker, the possibilities are almost endless. If you want, you can start at the very west edge of Champagne with a woman and her lunar calendar.

Krug Grand Cuvée

For the final two blends, we are moving up in price category to the most expensive Champagnes I will discuss in the book, at around $200 a bottle. I said earlier that you don't have to spend a lot of money in Champagne to drink great wine. And a $200 bottle of Champagne is not necessarily five times better than a $40 bottle. But just because there is no one-to-one relationship between price and quality does not mean that there is no relationship whatsoever. The real issue is that to make an exceptional Champagne requires exceptional resources and may cost an exceptional price. Samuel Johnson's observation comes to mind: "We grow to five feet pretty readily; but it is not so easy to grow to seven." These last two white Champagne blends show two different ways in which grapes help Champagne grow to seven feet.

Krug Grand Cuvée is a wine made every year, in which a little more than half of the blend comes from wines made in the current vintage, and the remainder comes from 120 to 200 separate reserve wines going back many years. The 169th edition, released in 2021, is composed of 43% Pinot Noir, 35% Chardonnay, and 22% Pinot Meunier. But while the varietal composition tells the story from one angle, it doesn't tell you anything about *which* grapes made it into the blend. And this is where Krug fills out an important piece of the Champagne puzzle.

There is a perception, somewhat understandable, that reputable growers who produce Champagne should be trusted to make Champagne from high-quality grapes; growers have a vested—often very personal—interest in growing, harvesting, and fermenting the best possible grapes for their wines. Large Champagne houses, on the other hand, may have little connection to vineyards and may be no more than bulk buyers of commodities. In this conception, large Champagne houses acquire grapes from growers something like the way shoppers buy fruit at the supermarket: they don't care much about who grew the fruit, and while they might give grapes a visual once-over, if grapes are not obviously defective, they chuck 'em in the cart and go. For some houses, this may not be too far from the truth, at least in consequence.

But for the houses mentioned in this book, the reality is quite different. The best houses seek out quality growers and often develop long-term associations with them. They don't only know how the vines are tended—they actually work with growers throughout the vintage to ensure that the raw materials for their products will be outstanding. And no house has better relationships with its growers than Krug, whose own vineyards supply only about a third of its needs. Some families have been supplying grapes to Krug for well over a century, and the tight bond extends beyond the growing season and harvest. Houses typically specify in their contracts with growers the village from which grapes will be sourced, but Krug's agreements identify particular vineyard parcels that it has determined grow the grapes that it wants. Grapes from every parcel from every grower are vinified separately and stored separately, resulting in 250 separate wines each year. Among other things, this allows Krug to invite its growers to taste wines from their vineyards, sometimes repeatedly as the wines age, to understand how the wines from their grapes have developed over time. The bond between Krug and the growers who have supplied the house and have helped build its reputation is a key indicator that the reputation will be earned again in each year to come.

Blending in Champagne reaches its apotheosis at Krug in the making of Grand Cuvée. There is no set formula for the percentage of grape varieties, though Pinot Noir is the lead grape, with Chardonnay not far behind, and Pinot Meunier in smaller doses. The task is to figure out the right combination among the 250 wines from the current vintage and the 150 wines from Krug's reserve library to express the house style in the context of the current year. Krug has to ensure that the final blend will satisfy both those who open Grand Cuvée upon release *and* the passionate devotees who evidently are intent on waiting to open Grand Cuvée at the last possible moment before they—not the wine—expire. Sounds easy, right? Krug Grand Cuvée is one of the few Champagnes that can do something—provoke an emotion—without ever being opened.

And what if you do open a bottle of Grand Cuvée? It's distinctively opulent. It's what I imagine it would be like in the dining car on the

Orient Express, or to have a room in your home that's been converted to a library, or a pair of bespoke brown leather shoes. It leaves footprints you can't erase. And yet, Grand Cuvée is fresh and luminous; it's classically Champagne. To compare Grand Cuvée to another wine would be unfair to both. It's inimitable. Admittedly, I have encountered some who do not prefer Krug, which I take as a hopeful sign that we all are still using our separate brains. But it's a wine that, if you can, you should drink so that you can discover where you stand. Although, if you find that you love Krug Grand Cuvée, you might begin engaging in strange behavior. Some years ago, I bought a few bottles of the edition from the 2003 base vintage, in recognition of the birth year of one of my sons. I am sure I will . . . open . . . a bottle . . . someday . . . maybe.

LOUIS ROEDERER CRISTAL

There is no better, more fascinating, example of the power of brand in Champagne than Cristal. With a wine like Pol Roger, it's very possible to miss the branding in the first place, and it's probably not too difficult to ignore once you become aware of it. But with Cristal, there is nowhere to hide and no path of escape. Cristal has become so much more than a wine. I would bet that a very small percentage of those for whom Cristal triggers any association with any concept or emotion could tell you a single thing about the wine itself, other than it is bubbly. And I also am confident that, no matter how knowledgeable and experienced with Cristal one may be, there are still stories about Cristal lurking in the background that affect the drinking experience. So instead of pretending that we are, or could be, above such influences, let's instead take a look at them and see what they contribute to this blend.

The story Roederer wants you to know is about royalty, wealth, exclusivity, and singularity. Tsar Alexander II of Russia loved Louis

Roederer Champagne and bought enormous quantities from the house. In 1876, he commissioned Roederer to make the best Champagne it could, exclusively for him, and packaged in a crystal, flat-bottomed bottle.* The Russian Revolution in 1917 was good for communists but bad for Roederer and Cristal. Fortunately, by 1945, Russian royalty had made something of a comeback—not in practice, of course, but in the nostalgic, emotional connections consumers made with an imagined luxurious past. In that year, Roederer made the first Cristal to be released commercially, launching a vintage wine that is the prestige cuvée of prestige cuvées.

But what makes the Cristal brand so interesting and instructive is that Roederer lost its grip on it. In the 1990s, Jay-Z and other hip-hop artists began calling out Cristal in their songs, reshaping Cristal's identity in the public's consciousness to some extent. By 2006, the connection between hip-hop culture and Cristal was so significant that a writer for *The Economist* wrote about it in an article entitled "Bubbles & Bling." But this caused yet more brand ambiguity, when Roederer managing director Frédéric Rouzaud made comments suggesting he wasn't thrilled with the Cristal/hip-hop connection. Jay-Z took great offense. And although Roederer attempted to clarify and backtrack, Jay-Z said he would never again support Cristal. Not every artist followed Jay-Z's lead, but the

---

* Legend has it that the unusual design elements of the bottle were inspired by the Tsar's fear of assassination. The fear was no paranoia—Alexander survived numerous attempts on his life, including a bombing of his carriage that he walked away from unharmed, only minutes before another revolutionary tossed a second bomb at his feet, killing him. Purportedly, the transparent bottle was designed to detect poison, and the flat bottom would prevent an enterprising killer from hiding a bomb in the bottle's punt. Whatever the truth of these tales, today's bottle maintains a connection with the original design and, thus, with the Tsar. No longer made of crystal, the glass is clear—yellow cellophane wrapping is necessary to protect the wine from the effects of light, and you shouldn't remove it during storage. The flat bottom thwarts both the hiding of bombs and the efficient storage of Cristal in cabinets that require the top of one bottle to extend into the punt of another.

episode left a mark, as the frequency of Cristal references in hip-hop music declined.*

The key takeaway is that, whatever you think of Cristal, you most likely have strong and well-defined beliefs about it. In this way, a bottle of Cristal does something to the drinker well before it is opened. Cristal triggers feelings, and these feelings will affect the drinking experience, perhaps immeasurably, but potentially as much as, or more than, the qualities of the wine itself. Although Cristal is the most obvious example of this principle at work, every other Champagne brand you know will sprinkle brand awareness into the blend. If you really want to understand and differentiate Champagnes, you'll have to consider—as well as you are able—what the brand means to you.

And as far that goes, let me add something to Cristal. Cristal's image should include that of a master farmer, unrelenting, meticulous, scientifically oriented, and uncompromising. Whereas Krug obtains superior grapes through its deep relationships with many exceptional growers, Cristal is produced entirely from grapes grown by Roederer, organically and biodynamically, mostly from old vines that yield fewer grapes of higher quality. I've discussed ripeness in this book, but ripeness is not the only factor that affects what grapes can do when made into Champagne. Not all ripe grapes are equally healthy, and the selection of grapes can make the difference between bad, mediocre, and outstanding Champagne. To maintain exacting standards in a vineyard and then select the best grapes requires not only will and expertise but also significant investments of money, time, and energy. But you, the drinker,

---

* Troy Ave's 2013 album *New York City* contains what I would judge to be the most perplexing Cristal reference as well as the most creative one. In "Cigar Smoke," he brags, "I only drink Cristal or Imperial Moet"—the video shows him holding bottles of both. It's a terribly misconceived boast, like claiming, "I only drive Ferrari or Toyota." But in my opinion, he hits it out of the park in "Show Me Love," when he taunts, "Man, fuck you / spit Cristal in your face / you can hate me now / and tell how success tastes."

can't be there during the growing season to watch any of the work or inspect the grapes. What it comes down to is this: who do you trust? If you had to bet on the quality of the plant material—which is, in fact, one of the bets you place when buying a bottle of Champagne—who would you entrust with your faith? Personally, based on its track record and what we know about its viticultural practices, I'll trust Roederer every day of the week.

Cristal is a blend of around 55% to 60% Pinot Noir and 40% to 45% Chardonnay from a single vintage. While it is aged on its lees for several years, Cristal does not see the most extensive lees aging you will find in Champagne. Cristal is not designed to be laden with yeasty flavors. It's not weighty or encumbered; it's not rich for Champagne. Cristal is Pinot Noir and Chardonnay blended to express purity, polish, and intensity. It's precise. More than anything else, Cristal is refined. It is a composite of materials that you can experience as having been fined, and re-fined, until they are a beam of light.

Some people stand at the rim of the Grand Canyon and think it's beautiful and grand. Others feel awe and interconnectedness. If you aren't in the second category, you may not be open to all that Cristal has to offer. Cristal is the kind of wine you can fully comprehend only when you are in a state of heightened purification and sensitivity, when you can feel the external and internal worlds most acutely, as if they are compressed into one. It's the Champagne you open on a temperate summer day, in a sun-drenched room, moments after your wedding. And if you turn to the back cover of this book, there I was.

Rosé

Rosé is a category of wine typically associated with summer, frivolity, and casual drinking. Provence, for example, churns out oceans of inexpensive still rosés admired more for their color than flavor. There are quite a number of consequential still rosés for those interested, but, for the most part, rosé is thought to be merely the cute, fun-loving, youngest child in the wine family.

Rosé Champagne occupies a different seat at the table. Because there are no red Champagnes, rosés are the only Champagnes markedly influenced by grape juice coming into contact with grape skins. They are at the end of the color and texture spectrums in Champagne, not in the middle of them. There is a wide range of styles and quality levels of rosé in Champagne. The wines that fail usually do so not because they lack character but because some attribute stands out too much—they are discordant. At their best, rosés maintain the characteristics valued in white Champagne—high acidity (though usually not as high as white Champagne) and subtle flavors from fruit and autolysis, adding aromas and texture from skin contact that contribute complexity but also are complementary. Unusually for a quality wine region, some of the greatest—and most expensive—Champagnes are rosés. The rosé versions of Cristal, Dom Pérignon, and Krug sell for around twice the price of the white cuvées.

The overwhelming majority of rosé Champagne is made by a method referred as *rosé d'assemblage*. The process is carried out in the same way as in the making of white Champagne, with one additional step. Before the fermented white wine is bottled, it is blended with anywhere from 5% to 20% of still red wine from Champagne. The red wine is almost always Pinot Noir, although there are some examples of rosés made with Pinot Meunier. The red wine is chosen for its delicate flavors and low concentration of tannins. The decisions of what red wine to blend and how much to include create yet more blending challenges and opportunities for the winemaker. It's notable that, throughout the wine world, it is very rare to blend white and red wines, and the procedure is prohibited for French still rosés. But in Champagne, this process is very sensible, because it allows winemakers to carefully control the perception of tannins in the final blend; nobody wants a markedly astringent Champagne.

A second way of making rosé Champagne, used less frequently, is the *rosé de saignée* method. *Saignée* means bleeding. Red grapes—typically Pinot Noir—are macerated on their skins in a tank for 24 to 48 hours, after which the colored juice is bled off the skins. The juice is then made into Champagne in the normal way. The reason this method is rare is that it is very easy to screw up. With the *assemblage* method, a winemaker can test blends of different red and white wines in different proportions and adjust as needed before settling on a formula. But with the *saignée* method, there is an element of unpredictability in how much color and, more importantly, tannin will be extracted from any particular batch of juice. The character of the tannin can vary too. Producers who make *saignée* rosés take risks; some don't pan out, and others are outstanding, characterful wines. Although *saignée* rosés are a small percentage of the total volume of rosés in Champagne, there are many of them on the market, especially from growers.

A third method is technically considered *saignée* but is a kind of hybrid. A small number of producers, most notably Louis Roederer, use the *saignée* method with Pinot Noir but then add Chardonnay wine to the blend. By blending in Chardonnay after Pinot Noir has been macerated, the winemaker can adjust color and tannins in *saignée* wines, while also making a more aromatically and texturally complex wine. Roederer's vintage rosé and its Cristal rosé are, in my opinion, two of the best rosé Champagnes on the market.

I love rosé Champagne. It's versatile, enchanting, and eminently drinkable. It's also a terribly misunderstood wine. If you think that rosé Champagne is feminine or at least not masculine, you aren't alone, but you are wrong. You'll have to get over that. Let's explore rosé Champagne with open minds, through the next four wines.

VILMART & CIE CUVÉE RUBIS

It is sometimes said that rosé Champagne is, in contrast to the typical still rosé, "serious." I get the point, but the description doesn't quite capture the essence of the comparison. The important difference lies in the degree to which your attention is captured by the quality of a wine. The real issue with so many still rosés is not that they are fruity, quaffable, and refreshing—what could be wrong with that?—but that they make low art of it. There are like silly puns: faintly amusing, but dull. The difference in Champagne is that rosés that are juicy and fruity—wines that would go down well five minutes after your morning alarm goes off—can still be engaging. You easily recognize these Champagnes as elevated. To take one example: Cuvée Rubis.

Vilmart & Cie is one of the finest and most conscientious growers in Champagne, and it makes a line of superior Champagnes. Cuvée Rubis is a non-vintage rosé made by the *assemblage* process; it's 90% Pinot Noir and 10% Chardonnay, with 15% of the Pinot Noir added in the form of red wine, giving it a salmon-pink color that is typical of rosé Champagne. Fermented and aged in large oak vessels, with malolactic conversion blocked, Cuvée Rubis is "serious," if it must be, in the sense that it is made to express Pinot Noir and Chardonnay in a Champagne with clarity, precision, and textural complexity. That some of the Pinot Noir is made into a still red wine first is no diminishment; to the contrary, it makes the Champagne more costly to produce. At the same time, this Champagne was not made for rumination. Cuvée Rubis is like a cherry-and-strawberry pie jacked up with red licorice, mint, and herbal tea. Its silky-soft texture complements these flavors, increasing the pleasure quotient. It's also crisp and light and not saturated. Cuvée Rubis is the kind of wine you serve at a party, and everyone asks where the hell you got it and, more urgently, whether you have more.

The large Champagne houses and many of the growers who export their Champagnes maintain websites in English that provide a range of details about how their wines are made, some more helpfully than others. They also offer descriptions of their wines, almost always unhelpfully; you could cut and paste these descriptions from the website of one producer to that of another, and nobody would know the difference. But there are gems here and there. Vilmart—I'm guessing the family business doesn't have a robust marketing department—calls Cuvée Rubis "a tribute to greediness." That's exactly right. Greediness has become synonymous with a selfish desire for more than one needs, but in 1828, Noah Webster defined the word as "Keenness of appetite for food or drink; ravenousness; voracity." For this kind of greediness, for its reward and relief, there is rosé Champagne, and there is Cuvée Rubis.

BÉRÊCHE ET FILS CAMPANIA REMENSIS

As I emphasize throughout this book, one of the strengths of Champagne, what makes the region endlessly fascinating, is how wines that are in large part so similar can also be so different. I hope you appreciate by now that the range of wines, even within a particular type of Champagne, is less like a series of dots on a line than it is a splatter of ink on paper. Rosés are like that too. Take Bérêche's Campania Remensis. Like Cuvée Rubis, it is made by the *assemblage* method and vinified in previously used oak, with malolactic conversion blocked. But Campania Remensis is, by stylistic design, dialed back, restrained. In Campania Remensis, only 5% of the total blend is red wine—compared to 15% in Cuvée Rubis and up to 20% in other rosés—and 30% of the blend is Chardonnay. The result is a lower intensity of color and fruit concentration. Where Cuvée Rubis receives a dosage of nine grams of sugar per liter, Campania Remensis is dosed with about three, a level that is just enough to prevent the wine from exhibiting bitterness. What you get in Campania Remensis is a wine that has plenty of character—in aromas, flavor, and texture—but that doesn't shout at you. It draws you into the glass and reveals its beauty in hushed tones. Campania Remensis is, in a word, elegant.

You might ask, what makes a wine elegant? An elegant wine pleases in its more minute beauties, chosen carefully to be arranged just so.

It's not merely that the wine's components are delicate, fine, pure, and tasteful, but that they are composed in a manner calculated to affect the sensitive, the discriminating. An elegant wine does not demand your full attention; it doesn't demand anything. But an elegant wine invites you to slow down, to savor, to gently interrupt streams of thought and notice what might otherwise be neglected. Campania Remensis is such a wine.

Campania Remensis also is Champagne that demonstrates the personal nature of taste. Not everyone is disposed to the elegant, to the subtle, to the curious—and there is nothing wrong with that. There are enough styles of rosé Champagne for just about every drinker and every occasion. And you if serve Campania Remensis to the wrong friend in the wrong place at the wrong time, and appreciation is not forthcoming, well, you'll need something more than elegance for the situation; let's hope you're graceful.

GEOFFROY ROSÉ DE SAIGNÉE

Sometimes a wine is so representative of a category and also such a high-quality example that you can shortcut your way to understanding what the category should be and can be if you simply try this one wine. That is the case with Geoffroy Rosé de Saignée. While the most well-known *saignée*-method rosé Champagne made entirely from Pinot Noir probably is Laurent-Perrier Cuvée Rosé, I think that Geoffroy's rosé is more typical of the style today. It's one of the more readily available grower rosé Champagnes, and I've yet to find anyone who doesn't like this wine.

It's that last point—the high level of appreciation for this wine—that is the real trick. *Saignée* rosés can be unusual, unbalanced, and, for some drinkers, unpleasant. The extraction of color from skins is one thing; these Champagnes are closer to salmon and red than pink. But it's the extraction of flavors and tannin in the process that is the potential hazard. Without expert management, a *saignée* rosé can be too bitter, or too dense, not refreshing, or lacking harmony in its fruity and autolytic components. Fortunately, a fair number of producers in Champagne get it right, and Geoffroy—here again the wine is from an esteemed grower-producer—dials it in expertly. First and foremost, Geoffroy's rosé is fresh and juicy, with bright, vivid flavors of red and blue fruits, and just a touch of spice. This wine is not aged very long on its lees, and the toasty character is subtle and doesn't compete with wine's fruitiness. Where some *saignée* rosés can be concentrated and heavy, Geoffroy's rosé manages to be concentrated and buoyant. It's robust and richly flavored, yet balanced and restrained. This is the key to the greatest *saignée* rosés, like Geoffroy's, making them not just highly pleasurable but also especially versatile. They're light and zippy enough to drink as an aperitif but have the substance and structure to stand up to just about any food.

One other note about this Champagne. You may have heard that rosés should be drunk young—aged on the truck and cracked open as soon as possible after leaving the store. There is decent logic behind this claim: put simply, some fruity aromas in wine will fade in bottle, and if the only value in a rosé is its fresh, fruity aromas, then holding the bottle for several years can deprive you of the intended appeal. Geoffroy actively encourages drinkers to consume its Rosé de Saignée young. I will say more later in the book about the question of how long you might age Champagne, but I want to point out now that many rosé Champagnes can drink very well for years and even decades after release. Perhaps as important, drinkers' preferences vary for the kinds of changes that happen in wines in bottle over time. What I think Geoffroy is doing is telling consumers that, to experience its rosé in the fruity style that Geoffroy conceived for the wine, it's best to drink it young. That makes some sense, though I have also enjoyed this rosé very much after several years of bottle age. I suppose my best advice is this: if you get your hands on a bottle of Geoffroy Rosé de Saignée, don't be concerned about its age. It isn't too young, and it hasn't expired. It's ready.

ANDRÉ JACQUART ROSÉ DE SAIGNÉE EXPERIENCE

If you really want to know a category, you've got to explore examples at the edges, where there is legitimate debate about whether someone has taken a concept too far. You need to check it out for yourself and decide: Is a Smart car a car or a Jack in the Box taco a taco? André Jacquart Rosé de Saignée might be one of those border cases. It's a big bad wolf. It's rosé taken not to the extreme—truly extreme examples are horrific—but to the limit of what is sensible in terms of extraction and concentration in Champagne. Not everyone will like it. But I do. And I'll tell you why.

This Champagne is made in the modified *saignée* method: 80% is Pinot Noir that macerates on its skins for 24 to 48 hours before being bled off and fermented in small Burgundy barrels, including 25% new oak (a high percentage for any Champagne). It is blended with 20% Chardonnay, also fermented in oak. Once bottled, the blend spends at least three years on its lees before it is disgorged. The result is a deeply colored ruby-red rosé that, from appearances, could be a meal. When you drink this rosé, you find out what happens when rosé Champagne is not just about ripe red fruits, spices, and bread—which this wine shows in high doses—but is also slightly bitter from tannin. Tannin gives the wine an unexpected, but very modest, grip that makes for a more robust and complex texture; the rough edge blends with creaminess and refreshing acidity in a way that is interesting, without making the wine unbalanced or unrecognizable as Champagne. There's a savory, peppered character to the wine too, giving it a stout flavor profile. Essentially, it's a wine that has just about every possible component you could throw into a rosé Champagne, with most of the levers pushed in the upward direction. It's not elegant, but it's not inelegant. This rosé is far too bold to be an aperitif. But it's a fascinating and delicious complement to rich foods—especially anything involving beef and, most especially, filet mignon. And any Champagne that works in this way is a winner in my book.

If you take away purely factual arguments, it's not so easy to explain why a Smart car is not a car, why a Jack in the Box taco is most probably or definitely a taco. It comes down to your gut feelings. My gut tells me that André Jacquart Rosé de Saignée Experience is not out of bounds. But once again, find out for yourself. My enthusiasm might suggest I think this Champagne—and all of the others described in this chapter—are wines everyone *should* like. But what I have tried to do instead is present twenty-two different high-quality Champagnes that expose countless facets of what the grapes of Champagne can do. If you pay attention to them, perhaps you'll notice how they strike you, from your personal perspective. That's what matters. Now, let's take another look at something else that may or may not matter: the differences between Champagnes produced by houses and those produced by growers.

CHAPTER 3

Interlude: Does Size Matter?

It's impossible to explore Champagne without getting drawn into the differences—real and imagined—between Champagne produced by large houses and those produced by smaller growers. That's because Champagne is a highly competitive marketplace, and your money is the prize. One point of product differentiation that is simple to communicate and understand is the size of the producer: Bottle A was made by a large, established, and wealthy Champagne house that has become a well-known brand; Bottle B was made a small family that owns a few acres of vines near its home and is recognized only by true Champagne aficionados. And the question you face is whether size matters. Specifically, whether smaller is better—whether you should seek out, buy, and drink grower Champagne instead of Champagne from one of the large houses. Unfortunately, much of what is said about the issue is confusing nonsense that only makes it harder for the drinker to understand and enjoy Champagne. As you might expect by now, I find this unacceptable. I want to you to have the greatest possible freedom to explore Champagne without unnecessary and screwy influences. So, in this chapter, I will try to separate the assertions about grower Champagne that are true and helpful from those that are false and useless. You can take it from there.

Let's start with an underlying cause of the problem: it is very challenging to sell grower Champagne in international markets. The worldwide market for Champagne sales is dominated by around a hundred large and medium-sized Champagne houses. Of these, about twenty-five not only sell huge quantities of Champagne each year (in some cases many millions of bottles) but also have become household names among wine drinkers—brands like Moët & Chandon, Dom Pérignon, Veuve Clicquot, Ruinart, Krug, Mumm, Pommery, Lanson, Laurent-Perrier, Pol Roger, Bollinger, Taittinger, and Louis Roederer. Their Champagnes are mainstays on restaurant wine lists and in retail outlets. Moreover, they have built moats around their brands through decades of heavy spending on glossy magazine ads, sponsorships, promotions, monstrous duty-free displays, and product placements at sporting events, in Hollywood movies, and in music videos. The famous Champagne houses have succeeded in associating themselves and their wines with prestige, glamour, power, success, and wealth—think Winston Churchill, Tsar Alexander II, and the monk Dom Pérignon, for example.

As I have pointed out already, the messaging from big Champagne houses is not very informative, often misleading, and mainly distracting from what curious Champagne explorers want to know: how a Champagne is made and what it delivers to someone who drinks it. But the messaging from large houses is distracting in a fairly transparent way for those who are truly interested in wine. It's silly, but mostly benign. Yes, your friends might be lured into buying Taittinger because it's featured in a Netflix comedy series, or Pol Roger because Winston Churchill drank it, and perhaps there is little we can do about that. But I'm guessing that if you're reading this book, you are the kind of person who will drink Taittinger or Pol Roger for reasons that have to do with the wines themselves.

Small grape growers and those who are in the business of trying to sell their wines—importers, distributors, retailers, restaurants—are in a very different market position from the one occupied by the big brands. They can't hope to have that level of brand recognition. And they can't sell the same story to the same customers. They have to sell a different idea to wine drinkers like you, who are inquisitive enough to seek out Champagnes beyond the big brands. Their story must be emotional, simple, effective, and easily transmitted through the chain of distribution and media. And in the early part of the 21st century, with anti-corporate sentiment on the rise, when the suffocation of mass urbanization has left many nostalgic for a simpler life on a family farm, and with the popularity of descriptions such as family-owned, artisanal, hand-crafted, limited-production, small-batch, and the like, a clear and potent idea to sell when it comes to grower Champagne is this: smaller is better.

Now, few will explicitly say that grower Champagne is, by its very definition, objectively better than large-house Champagne. That is too bold a lie. After all, anyone who drinks enough Champagne knows there are many great large-house Champagnes and many horrible grower Champagnes. There is no reason to believe, and nobody could seriously defend, the proposition that a family owning ten acres of vines should be expected—from these facts alone—to make Champagne of higher quality than a corporation that buys grapes from many growers over hundreds of acres of vines. Put another way, there is no evidence or logic to support a claim that there is an inverse relationship between a Champagne producer's size and the objective quality of its Champagne. No, what we are dealing with here are not outright lies or even knowing misrepresentations of the sort some large houses promote. We are dealing instead with suggestion that leads the listener to the conclusion that the speaker does not make explicit. We are dealing with bullshit.

We are told that small growers make Champagne that is genuine, authentic, expressive, honest, revealing, free of makeup; they make wines of terroir, wines made in the vineyard and not the cellar, wines that are not manipulated; they make wines first and Champagne second, whatever that means; they make Champagnes that manifest from the grower's unique position as a person of passion, humility, religiosity, devotion, creativity, and grace; in some sense, they don't make wines at all, but rather receive them from the earth and shepherd them through their natural transformation into Champagne. And of course, the large Champagne houses make no such wines and deserve no reverence, because they are corporate, faceless, detached, cold, mechanical, unimaginative, mercantile, uncaring, and, most damningly, conventional.

In his insightful book *On Bullshit*, Henry Frankfurt noted that bullshit is not necessarily true or false, and the bullshitter does not care about the truth or falsity of his statement. What distinguishes bullshit "is just this lack of connection to a concern with truth—the indifference to how things really are." The bullshitter says whatever suits his purpose, and if what he says sounds good and helps his cause, that's all that matters; truth, falsity, and whether the bullshitter believes any of his words are irrelevant. We could debate whether the self-serving platitudes about growers and grower Champagne or the caricatures of the large houses are true or false. But that would be pointless. What's important is merely to observe and be mindful of what is going on: somebody is trying very hard to sell you something.

With all of that said, there are some generalizations we can make about grower Champagne and how it often—but not always—differs from house Champagne that can inform our Champagne journeys. To be clear, I am speaking of the relatively small proportion of growers who have achieved the success of having their Champagnes distributed in key export markets, particularly the United States. It won't do us much good if we have to travel to France to drink a particular grower's Champagne.

In the first place, growers offer a much greater diversity of wines. It's not that house Champagne is formulaic or homogenous; very few consumers will ever drink through the entire range of styles and wines offered by all the top houses. But growers make Champagnes that the large houses have no interest in producing, because the market for certain styles of wine is simply too small. I referred to this phenomenon in the last chapter when discussing Françoise Bedel Dis, "Vin Secret," and that's just the tip of the iceberg. There are growers who produce *blanc de blancs* from villages that are known for Pinot Noir and growers who produce *blanc de noirs* from villages that are known for Chardonnay. Some treat Pinot Meunier as if it's the world's most prized grape variety, and others experiment with Chardonnay and Pinot Noir to make Champagnes that are incredibly surprising. Others blend grape varieties in uncommon proportions. Rosés would not have nearly the range they do if it were not for growers and their willingness to push boundaries, as you can see in the rosés discussed in Chapter 2. And perhaps most importantly, we wouldn't have any Champagnes made exclusively from grapes grown in lesser-known villages if it were not for the growers. I personally drink a disproportionately large share of grower Champagne, in part because I enjoy discovering what Champagne has to offer at its edges and in its nooks and crannies. You really can't know what you like if you haven't tasted broadly, and grower Champagne provides a way to experience the vastness of the tasting territory.

Somewhat relatedly, there is joy in the search for great grower Champagne. It's like a treasure hunt. Perhaps you hear something about a particular Champagne, and you think, *Maybe this will be wonderful and fascinating and special.* Of course, you can't find it on any shelf in any store nearby—they have the top sellers but not this Champagne. But you find a wine shop on the other side of the country that does have this potential treasure, and you have a bottle of this wine and some others sent to you. You store this bottle and forget about it for five years before remembering you have it and opening it. And then? I can tell you that I've felt genuinely fortunate that, somehow, I'd stumbled upon a particularly stunning grower Champagne that nobody I know has ever heard of, a wine that is no longer available for purchase because the few bottles that were produced sold out years ago. And I've felt that sense of appreciating the moment, in my kitchen, with this bottle, on this day, this evening, that will never repeat except in reflection. And I've even smiled about my inability to acquire more. More wasn't to be.

But sometimes you come up empty. You go through the same process of wanting, searching, finding, storing, and waiting, only to open the Champagne and—if you are honest with yourself—you're terribly disappointed. It feels bad. You don't just want your money back; you want your hopes and expectations and confidence back. And none will be returned. But in these situations—and I've been through many of them with grower Champagne—I figure it's part of the fabric of the grower Champagne treasure hunt. And besides, drinking disappointing wines and identifying what's wrong with them is part of the process of learning to appreciate great ones. Once again, we get back to diversity. The large Champagne houses don't make very many bad wines—there's too much market analysis and quality control for that to happen more than occasionally. They make great wines, good wines, and mediocre wines; the mediocre wines at the bottom of the pile don't have much to teach. What grower Champagne can give you, if you are willing, is a wild ride with ups and downs, twists and turns, filled with the unexpected, both pleasurable and not. Unless you happen to be extraordinarily lucky and only open the gems, you have to be in it for the whole ride.

What the large houses offer that the growers cannot is a reduction in doubt. The top houses relieve doubt about quality, styles, consistency, and availability. The importance of this fact cannot be overstated. There are times to take risks and times not to. If you want to be sure that you will drink excellent Champagne today and don't want to pay a fortune, go to your local wine shop, grab the basic brut non-vintage from Louis Roederer, Charles Heidsieck, Pol Roger, or Veuve Clicquot, to take a few examples, and go home delighted. And if you want to drink exceptional

Champagne today and don't care as much about the costs, there are even more options. I'm about as curious and experimental as Champagne explorers come; I like some weird wines. But I've never understood why that means I'm not supposed to enjoy Champagnes from established, large producers who always deliver quality, albeit in volume. We don't have to get so carried away with the different, the obscure, and the scarce that we deprive ourselves of whatever else there is that we actually enjoy. This is why I say again that the key to enjoying Champagne is to explore and experience it from your own clear perspective, not in the shadow of the judgments, opinions, lies, misrepresentations, and, yes, bullshit, of others.

Speaking of perspectives, there is no doubt that our feelings about a wine can be affected by what we know about who made it. If I handed you a glass of Champagne and told you it was made by a mass murderer, you probably would not enjoy the wine as much as if I told you the winemaker was a woman who devoted her life to charity. Less dramatically, as I mentioned early, Veuve Clicquot is a Champagne that is the same in every glass, but the reaction to it differs based on what the brand means to different drinkers. With growers, the situation is a little more complicated because there are not really two opposing perspectives. Who doesn't take some satisfaction in supporting small businesses and family businesses? Who doesn't feel a connection between themselves and a farmer they've read about—or even met—when eating or drinking something from that person's farm? Wines can taste better when they are made by people you like. This can't be measured objectively because different drinkers feel this emotional pull to different degrees. If you want to drink grower Champagne because you feel strongly about growers, you should do it. There is no reason to hold yourself back. My only suggestion is that you try to be mindful of what you are doing. If you lose perspective on your preferences and start believing there is something objectively better about grower Champagne, then you're apt to miss out on some of the wonders available to you.

Which brings me to the last matter I'll address on this subject. The entire exercise of trying to establish comprehensively and specifically who is better or best in Champagne is a march of futility and folly. Yes, we can be confident sometimes in saying that one Champagne producer consistently makes high-quality Champagnes more often than another producer. But that's not sufficient to resolve, or even hide, the ambiguities that make it impossible to score and rank producers. I suppose we could see if *U.S. News & World Report* would rank Champagne producers the way it does colleges. Perhaps a 2.4% weighting for the amount of chalk underneath a producer's vines would provide a measure of comfort to someone. But even it did, a more salient issue is that blanket statements that Champagnes from certain types of producers are always better than those from other types of producers ignore the fairly significant presence of the drinker and the drinker's experience in time. The Champagne I perceive as best right now may not strike you the same way and may not cause the same reaction in me tomorrow.

But the real folly in characterizations of the wines of one group of Champagne producers as better than those of others is that they assume the primacy of better. Ask yourself whether, in the various choices you make, large and small, you always seek the better or the best. I sometimes want to drink Champagnes that are, in objective respects, better than others, but I also at times seek out Champagnes that are novel, or different, or suitable, or interesting, or challenging, or enlightening. If you really want to assemble a complete picture of Champagne, as it appears from your personal perspective, you may conclude that different Champagne producers of different sizes have different pieces of the puzzle to offer. And ultimately it is in the piecing together of this puzzle that you are likely to find joy that no one type of producer or one viewpoint about producers can possibly provide.

CHAPTER 4

Drinking, Part 2:
Choices and Consequences

IN CHAPTER 2, I PLACED CHAMPAGNES into five categories: four categories of white Champagnes, consisting of three single-varietal categories and a category of grape variety blends; and a separate category for rosé Champagne, which requires the use of at least one black grape variety and may include Chardonnay. That's one way to classify and distinguish Champagnes. But as I pointed out in Chapter 1, there are so many choices available to be made in the vineyard and in the cellar, and so many distinct possible combinations of choices, that the potential for different Champagnes is almost endless. That is why the six *blanc de blancs* described in Chapter 2 differ from one another to such a great extent.

The question for the Champagne explorer is this: how detailed of a map do you need to have a working understanding of stylistic differences? How much do you really need to know—or should you know—about how a producer's choice at a particular step in the production process might affect a Champagne? At one end of the spectrum, it's easy to say that you should know that a producer's choice to make a Champagne either entirely of Chardonnay or entirely of Pinot Noir will result in two very different wines. If you want an extremely crisp, light, toasty Champagne with a subdued fruit profile of apples and lemons, you'll almost certainly be disappointed if you open a *blanc de noirs*. On the other hand, I can't imagine it would be worth any consumer's time to try to understand how the use of different strains of yeast might affect Champagne. While some might find this endeavor interesting, it's unlikely to be useful. That's partly because information about which yeast strains different producers use is not readily available and, more importantly, the choice of yeast isn't something you can easily observe in a glass and say to yourself, "I like what the yeast did here. I want to find more Champagnes that are made with the same yeast."

What factors are in the middle that are worth your while—the ones that are knowable, observable, and meaningful? There's no one answer, but I'll give you mine. In Chapter 2, I alluded to the potential effects of six choices: the extent of grape ripening; whether malolactic conversion is encouraged or blocked; the duration of lees aging; whether the Champagne is made from wines of a single vintage or blended from more than one vintage; the level of dosage; and whether the winemaker encourages some amount of oxygenation of the wine. The first three in this list are important. They can play significant roles in the overall composition of a Champagne, and I encourage you to notice how these factors affect the wines you drink. I will continue to mention them as they show up in other Champagnes in this book. But the last three factors—vintage or non-vintage, dosage, and oxygenation—require more explanation and, in some cases, account for vastly different styles of wines. In this chapter, I will take these factors in turn and illustrate a few points with four Champagnes for each.

Vintage or No?

We're accustomed to seeing all kinds of wines from all over the world that state a vintage year on the front label. If you look at the bottom shelf of the wine section at a supermarket, you will find still wines that cost a few dollars and display a vintage year (usually a recent year) on the front label. If the year stated on a label is 2020, for example, most wine drinkers probably would understand that this means the wine was made from grapes harvested in 2020, though many consumers likely are unaware that regulations typically do not insist that 100% of the grapes be harvested in that year. Vintage years may not be as informative as one might think, but they communicate something simple and roughly accurate in the universe of still wines: this wine was made in approximately the vintage year. The lack of a vintage designation on a wine label usually indicates that the wine is cheaply made and will drink like it.

Rows of Champagne bottles on retail shelves, however, look very different and are bound to cause confusion to consumers who are not well-informed. Most Champagne bottles do not bear a vintage year on the front label. Back labels vary widely in the information they provide, but most of them do not mention a year in any way. Of the small percentage of Champagnes that do display a vintage year on the front label, some may be expensive, but others are less expensive than some Champagnes without a vintage designation. For example, Krug Grand Cuvée and Laurent-Perrier Grand Siècle are blends from different vintages and are more expensive and more renowned than most vintage Champagnes. Various growers, in particular, produce vintage Champagnes that cost around the same as many non-vintage Champagnes made by large houses.

Adding to the confusion is that Champagnes without a vintage designation typically are referred to in advertising or marketing as "non-vintage" or "NV" Champagnes—though neither of these monikers will appear on a label. As I will explain, the English term "non-vintage" probably is not the best way to express the intended message from France. Meanwhile, restaurants usually use the "NV" designation, but others have chosen to replace it with "MV" for "multi-vintage"—an ill-conceived term that presumably was designed to rescue Champagnes from the humiliation of the "non" but in many cases is flatly inaccurate.

So that's the situation. Champagne is in the unusual position of being a wine region of very high esteem that overwhelmingly produces wines bearing no vintage designation. And there is no reason obvious to the consumer—such as quality or cost—why a small fraction of Champagne bottles are marked with a vintage year. Fortunately, the distinction between Champagnes that are and are not designated with a vintage is very straightforward, even if it also is in some respects unsatisfying. A bottle of Champagne may be labeled with a vintage year if it meets two requirements: (1) 100% of the grapes used to make the base wine were harvested in the stated vintage year; and (2) the Champagne is not released from the producer's cellar until at least three years from the date of *tirage*.

These requirements do not suggest that vintage Champagnes are *necessarily* superior to non-vintage Champagnes. There is nothing magical about the combination of a single vintage wine and three years of aging that automatically elevates the quality of a Champagne. What the two rules for vintage Champagne really do in combination is carve out a particular style of Champagne that is marginally more costly and risky to produce and less likely to be made into lower-quality, cheaper wines. Essentially, this is what the consumer might expect from vintage Champagne: a Champagne that, compared to non-vintage Champagne *usually* differs stylistically, *on average* is more costly, and *possibly, maybe, in many cases, but not in many others* is higher in quality.

Before we get to the four wines to discover how stylistic differences can play out, it's worth noting that a number of growers produce "non-vintage" wines that are made entirely from the grapes of one vintage. An example is Vouette et Sorbée Blanc d'Argile, discussed in the section on *blanc de blancs*. This is not technically a vintage Champagne and cannot be labeled as such, because it is aged for less than three years from the date of bottling. The reason growers often produce "non-vintage" Champagnes in this way is that, although they may use only the grapes from one harvest, either they do not want to incur the costs of extended bottle aging and wait over three years to sell their wines, or they may believe that shorter aging is appropriate for a particular Champagne. This is why "non-vintage" probably isn't the best choice of terms, as these Champagnes are best thought of as Champagnes "without vintage," meaning simply that they are not labeled with a vintage.* Obviously, it would be inaccurate to refer to Champagnes such as Blanc d'Argile as "multi-vintage," and I suppose we are stuck with "non-vintage," as inartful as that term may be. In any event, the vast majority of Champagnes are blends of wines from more than one vintage, and that leads us to our next wine.

Charles Heidsieck Brut Réserve

Reserve wines are critical in Champagne. As I mentioned in Chapter 1, reserve wines are those wines held back each year after the first fermentation, to be stored and aged for possible use in a future year's Champagne blend. Reserve wines serve three important purposes in Champagne. First, they provide insurance against poor vintages in Champagne's variable climate. If hail, frost, mildew, or lack of sun this year result in few healthy grapes, reserve wines from prior years can come to the rescue and allow a producer to make non-vintage Champagne by fashioning a blend of what is available this year and what has been stored from prior years. Reserve wines also allow producers to develop consistent house styles. Krug Grand Cuvée, for example, is not the exact same wine every year. But Krug's deep library of reserve wines allows it to create this Champagne blend from several different vintages every

---

* The back label, however, might indicate that the wine was made from a particular harvest, sometimes subtly. For example, a bottle of Vouette et Sorbée Blanc d'Argile from the 2012 harvest is inscribed with "R 12" on the back label.

year in a certain style and with a certain signature that is distinctive and continuous. By contrast, most Champagne houses do not produce vintage wines every year—they can't make and sell pricey wines that are worthy of the house's label some years. Even when vintage wines are made, they can push house styles out to the boundaries in unusual vintage years. This is a key reason why there are many more non-vintage than vintage Champagnes on the market.

The third important function of reserve wines lies in their potential—and here we uncover the brilliance of Charles Heidsieck Brut Réserve—to help make Champagne complex, layered, and aged, straight from a retail shelf to your glass, for around $50. Let's take a moment to be grateful for this "entry level" Champagne; it's not only a superb wine but also a wonderful example of what can happen when a producer makes a stylistic decision to employ older reserve wines generously.

Non-vintage Champagnes typically are composed of 40% to 60% of wines from the "base year" (the current year in which the blend is created), with the rest being reserve wines. In this respect, Charles Heidsieck's Champagne is typical—60% of the blend is wine from the base year, and 40% is reserve wines. But what is unusual for a moderately priced Champagne is the age of the reserve wines in this blend. In many non-vintage Champagnes, the reserve wines are composed completely of wine from the year prior to the base year. But in Charles Heidsieck Brut Réserve, the reserve wines range from five to fifteen years old, with an average age of ten years old. This results in a Champagne that is mellow, full-bodied, mouth-filling, concentrated, and developed upon release, with aromas and flavors tending toward dried fruits and coffee. It's soothing and warm, like a comfortable old leather chair. It gives the impression of richness in a way that calls to mind slow-cooked foods, and yet it delivers mouth-watering freshness. And the best part is that you can drink this Champagne and experience all of this right now, tonight, without aging it for a decade on your own dime. I'm not telling you that more or older reserve wines are always better; once again, it's a question of styles and preferences. But I am telling you—I suppose *imploring* is the better word—to try Charles Heidsieck Brut Réserve so that you can experience this classic style at an unreasonably favorable price.

Reserve wines come to the aid of the winemaker to save the day in poor vintages; they assist the winemaker to fashion a house style in every vintage; and in a Champagne like Charles Heidsieck Brut Réserve, they comfort the drinker, on a Friday night, having stopped at the store on the way home, and now relaxed, easing into a comfortable leather chair.

CHARLES HEIDSIECK BRUT MILLÉSIMÉ 2012

A good way to appreciate the differences between non-vintage and vintage Champagne is to compare two wines from a larger, established producer. The two Champagnes should seem as though they were born of the same family, sharing common traits; the variances should stand out at a distance as branches from the same tree. Assuming that is the case—and it is here with Charles Heidsieck—four main factors usually will influence the differences in style, though, of course, there are others and variations from producer to producer. First and most obvious, the non-vintage Champagne will contain reserve wines, and the vintage Champagne will not. Second, the grapes chosen for the vintage Champagne typically will be selected from higher-quality vineyards, will be more expensive, and will tend to accentuate vintage variation rather than obscure it. Third, Pinot Meunier usually is left out of the vintage blend. In this example, the Brut Réserve is composed of 20% Pinot Meunier, but there is none in the vintage Champagne. Fourth, the vintage Champagne will be aged on its lees much longer. Charles Heidsieck's 2012 vintage Champagne was aged on its lees for six years, compared to three for the Brut Réserve.

How do these differences in Champagne construction play out in the two Charles Heidsieck wines? Both have signature richness and freshness that is essential to the house's style, but the Réserve tilts noticeably toward richness and the vintage toward freshness and conspicuous acidity. In this context, where the vintage Champagne is racier and shows more purity of fruit, the toasty and slightly smoky flavors from longer lees aging are the perfect complement. The vintage wine is less layered but much more intense; it reaches out, grabs you by your shirt collar, and shakes the hell out of you from the moment you pour a glass and notice you can smell it from two feet away. The Réserve is a slow ride in an old Cadillac on a wide suburban parkway. The vintage Charles Heidsieck is power exhibited as speed, more of a Ferrari alone on a track.

Charles Heidsieck Brut Millésimé 2012 is not a wine you can ignore. It won't let you. That, at the end of it, is the real difference. I come back again to the importance of turning the camera around to the view of the drinker and asking not what a Champagne is, but what it does. Vintage Champagnes—the ones of quality that truly represent the style—are, in one way or another, arresting. They aren't made like the vast majority of Champagnes—carefully planned, consistent by design, and programmed for continuity. They are instead born of a winemaker's risk—to make a wine from the best fruit that can be found in one vintage, expose it for what it is without cover, let it sit on its lees for years, and then turn it loose. Under these circumstances, why would anyone expect a house's vintage and non-vintage Champagnes to have the same effect on the drinker? Charles Heidsieck's 2012 vintage Champagne is a wine that, much like an encounter with a fascinating personality, causes an interruption in thought—a spontaneous "holy shit." And then your wheels engage, you lean in, and you're drawn into the wine, as if it's drinking you. This is what vintage Champagne can do, to you, if you are receptive to it.

MOËT & CHANDON BRUT IMPÉRIAL

It's impossible to have a complete discussion about Champagne without a few words about Moët & Chandon. Moët owns more vineyards in Champagne than any other house, is the largest purchaser of grapes in Champagne, and produces approximately 10% of all bottles of Champagne. Its flagship wine, Brut Impérial, purportedly accounts for one out of every fifteen bottles of Champagne sold each year. This non-vintage Champagne is so ubiquitous worldwide that, for all practical purposes, it *is* Champagne in the minds of millions of consumers. Meanwhile, and probably for the same reason—its abundance—the acid test to confirm a person's Champagne snobbery of the worst kind is his or her belief that Brut Impérial is total crap. But for the person who genuinely wants to know Champagne, Brut Impérial is a valuable teacher.

Brut Impérial shows the effect of intentionally using fewer reserve wines and younger reserve wines—in contrast to Charles Heidsieck Brut Réserve. All else being equal, it is generally less expensive to produce a non-vintage blend with fewer and younger reserve wines. But that does not mean that the product will be inferior to a Champagne made from more and older reserve wines. Once again, we encounter intentional stylistic choices. Moët's Champagne is composed of only 20% to 30% reserve wines, and they are only one to three years old. This certainly is not because LVMH can't afford to use more or older reserve wines. Instead, the choice is made to satisfy a rather large market for this type of Champagne. Brut Impérial is intended to be light, fresh, and crisp; it is not meant to be rich and intense. Younger wines, in combination with relatively shorter lees aging, are critical to this style. This is a brunch Champagne; a wedding Champagne; a backyard-party Champagne; a dinner-party Champagne; a Champagne for toasting, laughing, and having a good time. It's a Champagne for just about everybody at just about any time. And once you understand this style, especially in comparison to a Champagne like Charles Heidsieck Brut Réserve, which is styled by older reserve wines, it's much easier to understand other non-vintage Champagnes by comparing them to both.

Still, you'll need your own personal reckoning with Brut Impérial's widespread availability, massive bottle count, and seemingly fine-tuned popularity. It's easy for the experienced Champagne drinker to regard Brut Impérial as barely off-dry, barely toasty, barely fruity, barely nutty, barely just about everything, and not enough of anything to deserve interest. But if you give it a chance, you might have to admit that it's classically Champagne. There is something to the wisdom of the public. If you ever want to point out what Champagne smells and tastes like to the uninitiated, you can do so reliably by handing over a glass of Brut Impérial. And contrary to what so many wine advertisements suggest, there is no logical relationship between scarcity and quality. There are plenty of growers who make tiny quantities of Champagne that are not even close to Brut Impérial by any objective measure of quality. My suggestion is this: try not to get so enamored with the special, the different, and the small that you cut yourself off from the enjoyment of the familiar and the commonplace. For myself, I'd rather not give up on cheeseburgers. And I know just the Champagne to drink with them.

Billecart-Salmon Cuvée Elizabeth Salmon Rosé 2008

Billecart-Salmon is unusual for a 200-year-old Champagne house, in that it is best known not for any of its white wines but for its non-vintage rosé. Pale colored, fruity but restrained, it's light and drinkable while still tasting like a grown-up's rosé. It's a standard on wine lists at nice restaurants, where it's priced in that upper-middle tier that can nudge your friends to say, "It must be very good" and, "Let's go for it." There is another rosé, however, that probably is not on the wine list, that definitely is not well known, and that is reasonably priced only in comparison to other rosés—Cristal comes to mind—that are truly profound: Billecart-Salmon Cuvée Elizabeth Salmon. It's a Champagne that demonstrates the capacity of vintage rosés made from outstanding fruit, carefully assembled, and aged an extraordinarily long time on their lees. But before I describe the wine further, I want to say a few things about vintage years—you may have noticed that I have called out Champagnes from 2012 and 2008 in this section—and how you might think about them.

Once you have in mind the idea of drinking vintage Champagne, the next questions are: *Which vintage years should I seek out?* and *Which ones should I avoid?* As you might expect by now, there are no answers that are correct or even helpful in every situation. That's because, in Champagne, there is so much variability among vineyards, variability among growers, variability among Champagne producers, and variability among wines. As an example, 2011 is regarded as a poor vintage (I'll get to why in a moment), while 2015 is considered to be far superior. But in *both* vintages, I have found certain Champagnes—particularly rosés, including non-vintage rosé Champagnes that were based on 2011 and 2015—that have had a distinctly off-putting vegetal element that ruins a wine. And yet, Louis Roederer's 2011 vintage rosé not only does not have this quality but is a Champagne that doesn't taste like it is from an inferior vintage in any way. Meanwhile, I've had expensive Champagnes from 2002 and 2008—considered to be two of the greatest vintages in recent decades—that ranged from disappointing to structurally unsound. All of this is simply to say that what makes a great vintage or a poor vintage in any year—for the wine drinker—is not the characteristics of the weather or the reported average quality of the wines, but the level of joy delivered by the particular wine the drinker is drinking right now. In an important sense, exploring vintages is just that—an exploration that you must take yourself and that probably will not result in total illumination. If you drink a Champagne that seems off in some way or is exceptionally wonderful, ask yourself, *What is going on in this wine?* Make a note of the vintage or the base year, and see if you find a pattern in other Champagnes. And if you don't want to do that, you could take a shortcut and drink anything Louis Roederer makes. Just saying.

However, if you'd rather play the averages: recent highly regarded vintages include 2012, 2008, 2002, and 1996; recent poorly regarded vintages include 2011, 2010, 2005, and 2001. In general, poor vintages involve uneven growing seasons and misfortune, particularly rain and rot at harvest. In 2011, the harvest was very early—premature, really—because the early part of the growing season was so hot, and it also rained in July; the result was too many underripe grapes and rot. Good growing seasons vary in character, and you might think that the absence of disasters would be their hallmark. But it's fascinating to read vintage reports in places like Burgundy and Champagne, where challenging weather is often part of the success story. A vintage report from Napa Valley can read like a description of the golden child: when she wasn't volunteering at the local food bank and winning competitions in three sports, she spent her youth achieving perfect grades in school and amassing the right friends; nobody was surprised when she became a highly respected diplomat—smooth sailing from end to end. But in Champagne in 2012, the unruly child did drugs, broke into houses, and skipped school during much of the growing season marred by spring frost, heavy rains, and lack of sun; yet just as he was about to get kicked out of school, the sun came out in August and stayed out, he turned his life around on a dime and got into medical school, and some perfectly ripened gripes led to vintage wines like Charles Heidsieck's. The kid became a heart surgeon.

The vintage of 2008 is considered outstanding mainly because growing conditions led not only to healthy fruit but also to base wines of high acidity, offering the potential—but not a guarantee—of greatness in Champagne. Billecart-Salmon is a house perfectly positioned for such a vintage, because it ferments base wines at low temperatures to produce fruity wines, which are more likely to shine with high acidity instead of falling into austerity. The 2008 Cuvée Elizabeth Salmon was made of 55% Pinot Noir and 45% Chardonnay, with 9% of the Pinot Noir vinified as red wine. It's a magnificent Champagne, notable in several respects. What's initially striking is the integration of the wine's components. Notice that this rosé was aged on its lees for ten years, but it is not hyper-autolytic. That's one mark of a beautiful vintage rosé: the yeasty notes are there, yet they have become so integrated with the fruit that they add subtle complexity and interest instead of standing out on their own. The texture is like satin, though it's not what you would call delicate, and it's not what you would call indelicate. It's attractive in the sense of being alluring. And, finally, the fruit character is different than in the rosés discussed in Chapter 2. Instead of the typical red fruit, it's blackberry and black currant, mixed with and subdued by citrus flavors from Chardonnay. The fruit is stunningly pure and compressed, like tiny diamonds. With high acidity from the 2008 vintage, the entire composition is stirring. Drinking this Champagne can change what you think about rosé, what it is, and what it can be. You cross the Rubicon; you can't return to the time when you didn't know great vintage rosé. And then you realize you asked for this. You opened the bottle.

You might ask, *Why are vintage rosés so expensive?* I am sure an economist could figure it out in the workings of supply and demand. But you don't need to read any charts to resolve this question. You can simply drink Billecart-Salmon Cuvée Elizabeth Salmon from the 2008 vintage and experience the answer instead.

Dosage and Delusion

Sugar is the foundation of wine, as it is converted into alcohol through fermentation. And sugar makes Champagne, through the second fermentation, when carbon dioxide is captured in the bottle. But it is the third role that sugar plays in Champagne—as dosage in the *liqueur d'expédition* before the cork seals the bottle for the last time—that can significantly affect a Champagne's style and quality. The amount of sugar included in the *liqueur d'expédition*, if any, is the result of the winemaker's intention to do one of three things with a bottle of

Champagne: to make it sweet, to make it balanced, or to make a point. I'll take these in order.

Sweet Champagne—Champagne with enough sugar added so that sweetness is a prominent feature of the wine—was popular long ago, but now the relatively small quantities produced typically are not made with the Champagne enthusiast in mind. Instead, sweet Champagne mainly is marketed for use in cocktails or—for some reason I've yet to apprehend—as a beverage to be poured over ice. If you want to explore sweet Champagnes, try Laurent-Perrier Harmony Demi-Sec, Louis Roederer Carte Blanche Demi-Sec, Moët & Chandon Ice Impérial, or, for one of the sweetest Champagnes you are likely to find, Veuve Clicquot Rich.

That's all I really have to say about sweet Champagne, because Champagne overwhelmingly is produced to conform to the modern consumer's preference that it be dry or slightly off-dry. To be clear about these terms: a dry Champagne may have sugar in it, but the amounts are too small to detect in the context of the particular wine; an off-dry Champagne has barely enough sugar to be noticeable, though you wouldn't consider the wine sweet. To some extent, drinkers can vary in whether they consider a particular Champagne dry or off-dry. For example, to my palate, Moët & Chandon Brut Impérial is off-dry. But it doesn't have a lot of residual sugar, and this Champagne may seem dry to you. What matters is that nobody would say Brut Impérial is sweet, and hence it conforms to what consumers expect from Champagne.

Assuming you are not attempting to drink a sweet Champagne, you'll need to know how to avoid it by correctly reading a Champagne label. The words used on Champagne labels to describe sweetness levels are somewhat confusing, and it's a strange case in which being fluent in the French language might actually put you at a disadvantage. For these reasons, I'm going to skip many of the details and summarize as follows:

If you see the word *Doux* on a label, you've found one of the rare very sweet Champagnes on the market.

If you see the word *Sec* on a label in any form—Extra Sec, Sec, Demi-Sec—the Champagne also is sweet.

If you see the word *Brut* on a label in any form—Brut Nature, Extra Brut, Brut—the Champagne is either dry or off-dry. These are the wines this book is about.

A Champagne labeled Brut Nature is not permitted to contain any dosage, and sometimes these Champagnes are labeled Zero Dosage. Technically, a wine labeled Brut or Extra Brut might contain no dosage. That's because these terms are permitted for use within ranges of sugar added to a Champagne, starting at zero. Brut Champagne can have zero to twelve grams of sugar per liter, while Extra Brut is a term that can be used for Champagne in the range of zero to six grams per liter. A small number of producers—Marie-Courtin is an example—label Champagnes that have no dosage Extra Brut. Fortunately, Champagnes labeled in this way are rare. What you can deduce almost every time a bottle is labeled Brut or Extra Brut is that the producer has added dosage for the second reason I mentioned: to make it balanced. It's worth understanding a bit about this aspect of Champagne production, if for no reason other than to stop worrying and learn to love dosage.

Some have suggested that dosage is like salt—an ingredient often added to food in small quantities not to make food salty but to bring out flavors and add balance. But we don't need analogies to understand dosage. Sugar is added to many different foods you wouldn't necessarily associate with sweetness, such as ketchup, canned soups, and peanut butter. Why? Because sugar interacts with other components to deliver a sense of balance and richness. In Champagne, sugar is a slight counterweight to acidity so intense that it could otherwise make Champagne seem unpleasantly tart. And sugar can react with amino acids in a process known as the Maillard reaction, contributing to the development of Champagne's nutty, toasted, and vanilla aromas. Finally, sugar is a preservative, and it is widely believed—though it has not been proven beyond doubt—that Champagnes lacking dosage do not age as well as Brut Champagne. It is for these good reasons that Champagne producers add very small amounts of sugar after disgorgement.

There is, however, no universally correct amount of dosage. What the Champagne maker must do is determine how much sugar should be included in a particular Champagne, based on numerous factors, such as vintage conditions, fruit ripeness, the age and proportion of reserve wines, the use of oak, and the intended style of the Champagne. For example, Charles Heidsieck Brut Réserve receives a slightly higher dosage than the Brut Millésimé 2012, because elevated dosage is consistent with the rich style of the non-vintage wine.

If you drank any of the Champagnes described so far in this book, did you notice how much sugar was added? I didn't. Drink a glass of Brut Champagne right now (you're not driving at the moment, right?), and see if you can determine from your sense of taste alone how many grams of sugar per liter of wine were added after the Champagne was disgorged. You can't do it? And was the Champagne dry or barely off-dry, but not so dry that you disliked the wine? Good. That means the winemaker—often through many internal trials of the same wine at different levels of dosage—did a fine job in determining how much dosage to add to your Champagne. It's best to think of dosage as one element of the blending process for each Champagne, an element that can't easily be extracted as a point of comparison. In other words, if you find a Champagne containing four grams of sugar per liter too austere, you can't assume that a different Champagne with the same amount of dosage—or even less—will strike you the same way. That's why my essential recommendation when it comes to dosage in Brut or Extra Brut Champagne is to not think much about it; drink good Champagne, and proper dosage will do its work in the background.

This brings me to those situations in which it may not be possible to ignore dosage—or, rather, the lack if it. The decision to make a Champagne without dosage sometimes is motivated, in significant part, by the desire for balance; certain Champagnes need no dosage and arguably would be unbalanced with added sugar. On the other hand, you don't have to look too hard to find Champagne producers who refuse to add dosage in the interest of making a point: that Champagne (or at least a particular Champagne) should not have any dosage. This position has circulated widely enough and gained sufficient consumer acceptance that several large producers who typically do add dosage to their Champagnes have included zero-dosage Champagnes in their offerings. The problem for the Champagne drinker is what you would expect when a wide range of producers making a wide range of wines all set a variable—one that we know affects a wine's balance—to the same number (zero): results vary. So, you will want to know if a Champagne has no dosage, but that fact alone will not tell you very much about the quality or style of the wine. What can you do to understand zero-dosage Champagnes, to avoid disappointments and poorly made Champagnes, and to find zero-dosage Champagnes that you will enjoy? Let's try to find out by looking at four zero-dosage Champagnes.

LAURENT-PERRIER ULTRA BRUT

You wouldn't know it by reading this book thus far, but I've poured many liters of Champagne down the drain in my kitchen sink. I hated these wines, usually not because they were awful but because I felt like an important promise wasn't kept. I haven't described any of those wines in this book. I figure if I'm going to illustrate points about Champagne, I might as well do it with wines I have enjoyed, wines that provoke my enthusiasm. Between these poles are Champagnes in a middle zone, Champagnes that I kind of like and kind of dislike. I'll drink a bottle if offered, but I have better things to do. I'm going to break the pattern here, because, while I don't love Laurent-Perrier Ultra Brut, I don't hate it either. And it is a very good example of a certain type of zero-dosage Champagne.

While other large Champagne houses only recently have launched Brut Nature Champagnes, Laurent-Perrier Ultra Brut has been on the market for forty years. It is prominently labeled Brut Nature and is produced in volumes that make it readily available. But consider a rather obvious difference between this non-vintage Champagne and Laurent-Perrier's basic non-vintage Brut Champagne, La Cuvée, which I discussed in Chapter 2. The latter receives dosage, but the level of dosage is not tied to a number that the house must use every year. In fact, it has changed over the years, trending down overall because there has been less need for it. But Ultra Brut gets zero every year, no matter what. In this way, Ultra Brut is a wine that is less likely to be balanced and, more to the point, is made in a style that emphasizes the lack of dosage. You will notice dosage—that is, the lack of it—in this Champagne.

In the glass, Ultra Brut smells much like La Cuvée. In the mouth, though, it's acidic to the point of being tart. The acidity grips and rattles your teeth. It's steely and pointed. It's light on fruit, and the mostly lemon flavor of this Champagne feels like an addition as opposed to a feature. And the wine is very drying. Dryness in wine is not a single state. There are levels of dry. This is as dry as dry Champagne gets. If you didn't know that Ultra Brut was deliberately made this way, you'd say it's wrong. It feels like being poked in the arm by the guy next to you on a plane, when all he has to do to avoid causing you to suffer is exercise a little care with the position of his elbow. All this Champagne needs is a little dosage. But that's not going to happen, because you're getting what you ordered: a wine that has no dosage and shows it. In that sense, there is nothing wrong with this wine. I don't prefer this style of Champagne, as you can tell, because there are plenty of Champagnes that don't poke me in the arm, and I don't see a place for it. Though I will say that Ultra Brut is camped in the decadent, delectable wing of the tart-and-dry Brut Nature party, which includes Champagnes seemingly designed to cater to voguish masochism.

I think you should try Ultra Brut. Maybe you'll love it—obviously, some drinkers do, or think they do. If you do, great. If not, you probably won't pour it down the sink. Either way, you will see for yourself the odd similarity between intentionally sweet Champagnes and certain zero-dosage Champagnes; in each case, dosage is the point.

AGRAPART & FILS VÉNUS

One day when I was a small child, my dental-hygienist mom decided that because sugar harms teeth, my siblings and I shouldn't have sugared cereals, soft drinks, candy, ice cream, or pretty much anything else kids dream of eating. This deprivation directly resulted in a man in his fifties who, in my wife's words, eats sweets "like a child." Oh, the irony. I did have one escape hatch back in the day. Crucially, my mom overlooked the sugar bowl, which presumably was intended for drawing off half-teaspoons for recipes demanding it. When she rushed off to work, I dumped the stuff all over my breakfast of bland cereal or grapefruit. As early as the second grade, I was slicing grapefruits in half and spreading granulated goodness over the top of the fruit, which I deemed too bitter. Later in life, I realized that the grapefruits of my childhood were underripe. Grapefruits have plenty of sugar, but they don't taste sweet because, unlike other fruits with the same amount of sugar, grapefruits also can be very bitter. Ripe grapefruits have enough sweetness to balance and suppress bitterness so that it is not such a prominent feature of the fruit. This results in a delicious grapefruit; no table sugar required.

In a similar way, delicious zero-dosage Champagnes are made from fruit so ripe that the sweetness in the fruit is sufficient, without dosage, to make for a balanced, harmonious wine. Agrapart is one of the most thoughtful, careful growers in Champagne, emphasizing fruit ripeness and quality from old vines. Vénus is a vintage *blanc de blancs* made from Chardonnay vines planted in a tiny parcel on the mid-slope of a single vineyard in the Grand Cru village of Avize. It receives no dosage, but you wouldn't know it from drinking the wine. It's a vivid, intense Champagne filled with flavors of citrus (yes, I detect grapefruit), almonds, and yeastiness, with a fine-grained texture. It exhibits a lemon-pie quality, and the baker didn't forget to dollop cream on top. It screams acidity and fruitiness simultaneously, and you're perfectly happy that the screaming goes on and on. There is nothing out of harmony, nothing sticking out obtrusively. This wine isn't great because it lacks dosage. It's great because it is the definition of balance, expressiveness, and clarity in Champagne.

Now, compare Vénus to another Agrapart vintage *blanc de blancs*, Avizoise. It too is made from Chardonnay grown in Avize, though the fruit comes from two different vineyards to the northwest of the source for Vénus. The flavor profile and texture of Avizoise are different. What is not different is Avizoise's coherence and brightness; that it is gripping and captivating; that it is neither too rich nor too lean. Here's the kicker: Avizoise receives three grams of sugar per liter for dosage. It's a very small amount of sugar, so close to zero and yet not zero. You have to assume Pascal Agrapart decided this modest addition is necessary. And though we can't perform dosage trials for ourselves to see what would happen to Avizoise if it had no dosage, the Champagne Agrapart did make speaks for itself. To my mind, Agrapart's Champagnes are exactly what low- and no-dosage Champagnes should be. They are Champagnes that, like Brut Champagnes with higher dosage, receive the right amount of dosage, which might be zero but might be a little sprinkle of sugar from the bowl. So little that mom won't know it's gone; enough to put the wine and the drinker in just the right place.

MARIE-COURTIN EFFLORESCENCE

Down in the Côte des Bar, Dominique Moreau operates a fairly young estate named after her grandmother. She has a modest amount of vines and decidedly big ideas. She makes a series of Champagnes, each of which is produced from a single grape variety and from one vintage. She grows grapes organically and biodynamically, makes her own compost, and uses only natural yeasts in the production of her wines. That's just the tip of the iceberg; according to her distributor, she is guided in her grape growing and winemaking not by well-worn, vague notions of spirituality but by the swaying of pendulums, back and forth, to help her read energy and figure out what to do. She thoughtfully names her wines—Concordance, Efflorescence, Resonance, for example—to reflect what she sees as intrinsic characteristics, though they may be imperceivable to everyone else. And, as you might expect, she makes all of her Champagnes without dosage.

I mention Marie-Courtin here because I find these Champagnes, particularly those made from Pinot Noir, to be thrilling, intriguing, and intense. In Efflorescence, Pinot Noir is fruity, barrel-influenced, remarkably Burgundian in flavor, and yet classically Champagne in mouthfeel. The fine mousse and light pastry aroma contribute to a sense that the Champagne is at once natural and sophisticated. And while I think Marie-Courtin's *blanc de blancs*, Eloquence, staggers a bit without dosage around a thin line that separates the austere from the pleasant, Efflorescence's ripe, rich fruit leaves no doubt that the wine has everything it needs and lacks for nothing.

I also mention Marie-Courtin because in the game—the one in which a grower tries to make a mark through producing outstanding zero-dosage Champagnes—Marie-Courtin wins. Unfortunately, the whole category of zero-dosage Champagnes made by growers are rather like your eight-year-old's soccer league, where not everyone wins—did you watch the games?—but everyone takes home a trophy. This is achieved through good old-fashioned wine bullshit, where you take something you know the big houses won't do without and turn it into an ethical or moral issue. Everybody knows sugar is bad for humans—take it away, and their skin clears up, their fat bodies get less fat, and they hold out longer in nursing homes. Why not say Champagnes are better without it too? It sounds just good enough to sell. And, therefore, you will hear people who appear to be serious claim that growers' zero-dosage wines—nobody is talking about large house wines like Ultra Brut here—are superior categorically because they are cleaner, more pure, honest, natural, transparent, and authentic; they better express the grape variety's innate characteristics as well as those of the vineyard or, to the extent anyone notices the difference, terroir, the soil, and the place; they don't mask anything because—and this common reference to facial skin is perhaps my favorite—they don't wear any "makeup."

It would be simple enough if all of this really were about whether Champagne is defiled beyond redemption by a few lousy grams of sugar. But the issue is bigger than that. It's an extreme offshoot of the selling of grower Champagne, where growers who specialize in zero-dosage Champagnes are even closer to godliness than those who don't. As a drinker, the theater of it all is dissatisfying. On the one hand, zero-dosage Champagnes can seem painstakingly bohemian—a phony attempt to eliminate phoniness. And yet that criticism can itself sound phony—where the speaker reflexively claims to know better than those who think they know. My suggestion for dealing with this nonsense is to not get taken in by the dramatic play that involves a series of play-ers—winemakers, wine sellers, writers, drinkers—who argue endlessly about the merits of zero dosage until the lights go out. Just see about the Champagnes. They don't have personas, and they don't have political or economic positions. They're just wines that either are enjoyable or are not. There is a certain liberty in that for the drinker. Personally, I'm not interested in joining some quasi-religion in Champagne, nor do I feel compelled to avoid Champagnes promoted by the religion as a matter of course. I just want to drink delicious Champagnes, damn it. And that is how I came to recommend to you zero-dosage Champagnes made by Vouette et Sorbée, Agrapart, and Marie-Courtin. If you want to groove with makeup banishing, or pendulum swinging, or soil munching, for whatever reasons, by all means, have at it. Otherwise, it really is fine to ignore the dosage debate going on outside of your glass and, if you can, enjoy what's in it.

TARLANT ROSÉ ZERO

Zero-dosage rosés are rare in Champagne. Tannin from red wine can add bitterness to rosés, providing another reason to add sugar for balance. In fact, rosé Champagnes typically have slightly higher levels of dosage than white Champagnes to account for this difference. To take dosage down to zero in a rosé invites disaster. A drying, bitter, harsh rosé Champagne would seem to miss the point. This is why Tarlant's Rosé Zero stands out, and it offers a good lesson as well.

Benoît Tarlant's family has been growing vines in Champagne since the seventeenth century and began making Champagne from the estate's grapes almost a hundred years ago. Facts of this sort are thrown around in the world of wine to suggest something—I'm not always sure what. Maybe it's that the grape grower or winemaker is traditional, or deep rooted, or experienced. But at least in the case of Tarlant, what the long history of success reveals is a commitment to innovation. It's the willingness to look years ahead by doing trials today, to try something new, see what happens, and then try something else when the wine you created isn't the best you think it can be. Tarlant began making zero-dosage Champagnes before it was trendy, but today's Tarlant Champagnes aren't just copies of the wines made in decades past. Rosé Zero is a Champagne twenty years in the making, with the formula having changed over time in an effort to improve the wine. It's a Chardonnay-dominant rosé, but less so than it was in the past. A key to the success of the current version of this rosé is blending Chardonnay with red wine made from very ripe Pinot Noir and aged in barrel, making tannins less harsh and bitter on the palate. The result is a rosé that is perfumed and delicate, light and fruity, soft and refreshing. It's a beautiful rosé Champagne that was designed from the ground up to lack dosage, as opposed to Champagnes in which the dosage is simply left out.

Put another way, Rosé Zero's excellence is the product not only of conscientious grape growing but also of expert winemaking—a fact inconveniently inconsistent with the romantic notion that zero-dosage wines are more natural, less manipulated. If you can make a rosé Champagne, it's easy to make it without dosage—just don't add sugar. But, evidently, it's not so easy to make one without dosage that many consumers would want to drink. And this crucial distinction brings us to answer the questions I posed at the beginning of the discussion, which can be summarized as follows: *How does a drinker find good zero-dosage Champagnes and avoid bad ones?* I've suggested already that one answer is that you don't; you're better off simply drinking quality Champagnes irrespective of how many grams of sugar, if any, were added to the wine. And the other answer provided by Tarlant's example is that, if you are intent on drinking zero-dosage Champagnes, buy from producers who make great Champagnes first and zero-dosage Champagnes second. Withholding dosage does not make mediocre Champagne better; it just makes it drier. It's only from the right hands that a Champagne like Rosé Zero appears. And it is in thinking about dosage this way that I believe the comparison to salt as a finishing touch in a dish is a good one. For with Champagne, as it is in cooking, it is very difficult to say for sure exactly how many grains—perhaps none?—should be sprinkled at last. But the better chef, or in Champagne the *chef de cave*, knows best.

Oxidative or Reductive

You and a group of your friends are at a restaurant—the cuisine could be Chinese, or Indian, or Mexican—and at some point the waiter asks the question you've heard many times: "How spicy do you like it?" Everyone looks around, and you know there is no single answer that fits all preferences, both fixed and the ones that happen to be percolating at the moment. Peppers burn your tongue, and the amount of burning affects the overall experience of eating whatever food pepper has been added to. Everyone would agree that at some level of pepper addition the burning would be so great as to ruin a meal—peppers would prevent you from picking up the character of anything else and would make eating unpleasant. But in between are innumerable levels of spicy (starting with completely bland) that speak to matters of personal taste or whatever moves you. The analogy to oxygen in Champagne is not perfect for several reasons, but it gives you an idea of what is going on. How much oxygen a Champagne producer allowed into its Champagne will affect the wine's aroma and flavor profile in ways that can activate drinkers' preferences; like spiciness in food, oxygen in Champagne has a greater effect at higher doses, at some level ruining the wine even for those who prefer oxidative Champagnes.

Whether to make a Champagne that is influenced by oxygen and by how much are stylistic choices made by each producer in advance of producing Champagne. There is no way to completely prevent the introduction of oxygen into Champagne; pressing, disgorgement, and the permeability of corks mean that every Champagne will be at least slightly, though perhaps imperceptibly, oxidative. But Champagne producers can take steps to avoid oxygen—principally by fermenting and storing wines in stainless-steel tanks—to such an extent that their Champagnes do not reflect the characteristics that oxygen can deliver. These Champagnes are referred to as being reductive. Oxidative Champagnes reveal the influence of oxygen in the glass and usually are fermented or stored in oak vessels. Oak barrels are porous, and this allows for micro-oxygenation—the introduction of very small amounts of oxygen into the wine. Most Champagnes are neither very reductive nor very oxidative, but Champagnes usually will at least lean one way or the other.

What does it mean to a drinker if a Champagne is reductive or oxidative? Take a green apple, and cut off a slice. Smell the apple where you made the cut. The aromas are fresh and vibrant. The smell is mouth-watering. You can imagine the apple would be tangy if you were to bite into it, that you would taste green apple in its most pure form. To a great extent, reductive Champagnes, especially those that have not undergone long lees aging, are characterized by fresh, vivid fruit. If you look back at Chapter 2, Ruinart Blanc de Blancs and Laurent-Perrier La Cuvée are prime examples of very reductive Champagnes, in which the fruit aromas are clear and pristine. There is more to reductive Champagnes than this, as we will see below. But for the most part, producers who make reductive Champagnes are trying less to add something to Champagne than to prevent oxidation from adulterating their wines.

Wait two or three hours, and smell the cut-open apple again. It still smells like a green apple, but oxygen has dampened the fresh fruit aromas. The apple smells more like applesauce or dried apple, with a degree of nuttiness. If you have any synesthetic tendencies, you might say that the apple now smells darker or is lower toned. If you are familiar with Oloroso Sherry, you understand well what oxidation can do to wine, in that case developing aromas of hazelnuts, walnuts, toffee, and caramel from a neutral grape variety. Few Champagnes come anywhere near this level of oxidation, but producers who make oxidative Champagnes believe that oxidation provides aromas such as dried fruits and nuts that add complexity to Champagne. Krug Grand Cuvée, discussed in Chapter 2, is on the oxidative side of the ledger.

You will need to do some investigation to figure out whether a particular bottle of Champagne is reductive or oxidative. There are no labeling terms that will assist you, nothing you can discern from looking at a bottle. The terms "oxidative" and "reductive" will not be found on producers' websites. Professional reviewers sometimes use these terms and sometimes use words associated with them. One way to get a rough idea about a Champagne is to find out whether and how extensively a producer uses oak. But the very best way to get a grip on this issue, and my favorite way, is to drink a few bottles of Champagne. To start, I'll tell you about four.

JACQUESSON 700-SERIES

For any drinker who wants to explore the oxidative style of Champagne without hitting extremes in price or quality, I know of no better place to start than with Jacquesson's 700-series Champagnes. But before we get to that, there is something else that is unusual and interesting about these wines that takes us back to the discussion of vintage and non-vintage Champagnes.

Non-vintage Champagnes, especially from the large houses, are consistent from year to year. Yes, slightly tweaked here and there every once in a while, but not so much that most drinkers would notice. If you enjoyed Pol Roger Brut Réserve a couple of years ago at a restaurant in Orlando, well, you can and should be confident that you'll be drinking the same Champagne when you grab a bottle at a wine shop today in Minneapolis. Non-vintage Champagnes from the big brands develop followings and are somewhat like your favorite blended malt whisky: it had better taste the same in every place and every time, or there'll be trouble. Vintage wines are made in a certain style, but they will reflect the conditions of the vintage year, and it's understood they will vary by some measure. Notice the tension here: every year, the houses would like to make spectacular vintage wines, but they also must make consistent non-vintage wines, and there are only so many grapes and reserve wines to push one way or another and make both Champagnes happen. That's just the way it is.

Though, does it have to be? Jacquesson is an old Champagne house that has seen its ups and downs over the last two centuries and more. Through changes in ownership and fortunes, what had not changed as the 20th century closed was that Jacquesson dutifully produced a non-vintage Champagne that was consistent in style each year and a vintage wine every year it could. But one year, the brothers who now own Jacquesson realized that the traditional two-Champagnes scheme meant that they never made the single best wine that they could. And they thought, *Why not do that every year instead?* The non-vintage and vintage Champagnes were dropped, and the 700-series was born, based first on the 2000 vintage and numbered 728. Each year, a new Champagne with the next number is released, and right now I'm taking my time drinking 740, based on the 2012 vintage. Year over year, there is no consistency in the mix of grape varieties, the amount of dosage (though it is always low), or the percentage of reserve wines used. Each 700 wine is different, and it's difficult to describe the entire series in precise terms.

Yet, the 700-series Champagnes are made by the same winemakers in the same winery, and it's not the point of the series to blow everyone's mind every year with something completely unfamiliar. If there is one characteristic you cannot miss every year, it is that the 700-series Champagnes are oxidative. Vinified and aged in large oak casks designed for micro-oxygenation, Jacquesson's Champagnes exemplify the oxidative style—at a high level of quality—in Champagne. These Champagnes show fruit character, for sure. But the fruit is shaped and colored by oxygen in the way that your cut-open apple was after a while. It's rounder, shaded. It's like tossing fruit, almonds, and hazelnuts in your mouth at the same time. The overall impression is of warmth. Not the kind of warmth you get from sun in July, but from wearing a sweater while walking through an apple orchard in October, or sitting by a fire on a cold night. Oxidative Champagnes aren't one-dimensional, of course. We're talking about one element of style. The 700-series Champagnes also are very refreshing, long, and marked by a hint of salinity. But the oxidative component is a thread you will want to recognize in Champagne and ask yourself what you think. Not everyone will enjoy this style, while others are crazy about it. I love oxidative Champagnes, up to my own personal edge, which Jacquesson's 700-series Champagnes have never tipped over.

There is something else consistent about the 700-series Champagnes. It's consistently fun to open the next numbered bottle and find out what's inside. At a time when wine is so thoughtfully styled, so heavily brand-based, with brand development, brand messaging, brand awareness, brand ambassadors, brand this, and brand that, it's refreshing when a Champagne's brand—if one could call it that—is essentially, "We'll make the best non-vintage Champagne we can each year; hopefully, you'll like it." I've liked every one I've drunk so far; though if I ever don't, there's always next year.

BOLLINGER SPECIAL CUVÉE

Speaking of brands, Bollinger is the Official Champagne of James Bond and MGM's latest Bond film *No Time to Die*. Bollinger says so right there on an otherwise useless, flimsy promotional carton containing a bottle of its entry-level Champagne, Special Cuvée. Bollinger has placed its Champagnes into every Bond movie since 1979, completely displacing Taittinger and what sure seemed to be 007's favorite Champagne before *Moonraker*—Dom Pérignon. It's a testament to the powers of branding and marketing that you can find wine writers attempting to explain that James Bond's choice of Bollinger Champagne (as if the character actually did the choosing) was a fine one, or that it suits him, or that Bollinger Champagne and James Bond share certain characteristics. It's all good fun, no doubt. Though you have to wonder sometimes how far we are willing to follow promotional nonsense and detach ourselves from the actual, present, personal experience of drinking wine. Especially after the unsatisfying films made in the '90s. I really don't know.

But about the wine. Bollinger Special Cuvée is a basic non-vintage Brut Champagne that is produced in high volumes and competes with similarly priced Champagnes from the other very large houses. In this crowd, it's distinctive. Until fairly recently, it might have been too distinctive: Special Cuvée was considered quite oxidative, to the point that it probably turned off a good number of Champagne drinkers. It has become less oxidative in the last decade, as Bollinger instituted practices to prevent unwanted oxidation, while still maintaining a style that shows the effect of gentle, controlled oxidation more than any other non-vintage Brut Champagne in its class. Approximately a quarter of the wine is fermented and aged in old oak barrels, and around 50% of the blend is composed of reserve wines.

When you compare this Champagne to Jacquesson's 700-series, the oxidative character is somewhat tame. The cut-open apple hasn't sat on the counter as long. But line it up with Moët Brut Impérial or Laurent Perrier La Cuvée, and you will notice significant differences from the effects of oak. The first of these is the complexity of flavors from mild oxidation: dried fruit, almonds, but also sweeter flavors than you find in Jacquesson, such as toffee and caramel. Bollinger Special Cuvée also is spicy, tasting of cinnamon or cloves, or what I experience as the taste of graham crackers. And oak affects Special Cuvée's texture, giving a round, soft impression on the palate, as if the wine rolls slickly around your mouth.

Oak plays a critical role in making Bollinger Special Cuvée old-school Champagne in modern clothes. The high proportion of Pinot Noir in the blend (60%) and the significant use of reserve wines contribute to the effect. It's fresh and vibrant and clean, but the oxidative, spicy, round elements make it rich. There's another side to the purity-of-fruit conversation, a side of Champagne that is appropriately modern but hasn't been so thoroughly chiseled and scrubbed and streamlined that a slice of the Champagne of yesterday is lost. Bollinger Special Cuvée is a reference Champagne. How spicy do you like it? Try this Champagne and begin to find out.

Dom Pérignon

What is Dom Pérignon? For some, Dom Pérignon is the definition of Champagne. I would bet that if you asked a person who knows nothing about wine to name one Champagne, the response would be "Dom Pérignon." For others—those who are vaguely aware that there is a luxury segment of Champagne—Dom Pérignon defines that category of Champagne too. Naturally, this means that there is a sizable segment of wine drinkers, sufficiently self-assured, who are comfortably certain that Dom Pérignon is a widely overrated popular icon; they can name three superior Champagnes right now, they might promise. In other words, Dom Pérignon is less of a wine than it is an abstraction, a symbol, a concept of one type or another. And, admittedly, Dom Pérignon means something apart from the taste of the wine to me too. But before I get to that, there is one thing we can say for sure about Dom Pérignon: it is an excellent example of long-aged reductive Champagne.

Dom Pérignon is fermented in stainless-steel tanks, and care is taken from then on to avoid contact between wine and oxygen. As with other reductive Champagnes, such as La Cuvée, Dom Pérignon lacks oxidative aromas that might suppress fresh, fruity aromas; you typically will not find in Dom Pérignon aromas of nuts, spices, dried fruits, or apples sitting cut-open on the kitchen counter for hours. But this is where any similarities between Dom Pérignon and the flavor profiles of younger reductive Champagnes end. That's because Dom Pérignon is aged at least eight years and is characterized not merely by the absence of oxidative aromas but also by the development of additional, reductive aromas that are hallmarks of this characterful wine. Coffee is the most prominent to my nose, followed by cocoa powder and a very subtle yet noticeable note of peat smoke. Peat smoke isn't an aroma normally associated with wine, so call it the smell of earth and moss on a damp, foggy day, with a campfire burning nearby, mixed in with a slightly medicinal odor. Or drink a lot of peated whiskies and call it peat smoke. Either way, the point is that Dom Pérignon takes reductive Champagne for a long haul, and it picks up complexity from aromas that are completely different than those found in oxidative Champagnes.

What's also interesting about Dom Pérignon is that these developed flavors exist in a wine that is, even at an older age, very reductive in a textural sense as well. Where oxidative Champagnes can feel weighty on the palate, Dom Pérignon is light and airy. In my view, this ethereal texture is one reason why Dom Pérignon and other reductive Champagnes work so well as aperitifs. No matter how complex they may be in aromas and flavors, they don't impose any demands on the drinker. They don't pair with food as naturally as oxidative Champagnes and don't send the signal that you should be eating food. You can hang out and drink them.

Of course, breaking Dom Pérignon down into attributes and describing it in technical wine terms teaches us something about Champagne, but it doesn't tell us what Dom Pérignon is either. At the end of it, trying to define Dom Pérignon once and for all is like trying to explain the meaning of life. It is what you think it is. To me, Dom Pérignon is joy. When I smell a wine that I perceive as not merely great but grand, I almost always feel comforting joy, immediately followed by wistful sadness. Somehow the peak experience highlights the impermanence of the moment, of the wine, and of everything. Strangely, I've never experienced the other side of joy when drinking Dom Pérignon. Maybe it's because I know there are millions of bottles in circulation and more are coming; maybe it's because I'm too fascinated to be distracted. And maybe it's because I tell myself sorrow isn't appropriate when I'm holding a glass of Dom Pérignon, that it's right to feel instead the emotion excited by good fortune. I'm not sure. I only know that Dom Pérignon is, in this way, not just a wine to me but a relief. And if it's not just a wine to you, I ask you, what is Dom Pérignon?

LAURENT-PERRIER CUVÉE ROSÉ

Laurent-Perrier Cuvée Rosé purportedly is the world's best-selling rosé Champagne, and it isn't difficult to understand why. It's about as juicy and fruity as Kool-Aid, with the freshest of cherry, strawberry, and raspberry flavors. This is a Champagne that not only avoids any hint of oxidative aromas but also preserves primary fruit and floral notes seemingly to the maximum extent possible. It's lively and light on the palate, making it dangerously quaffable. It's as close as Champagne gets to avoiding the impression of an alcoholic beverage, much in the way of many still rosés. Fundamentally, Cuvée Rosé is uncomplicated—you might say simple. It's a crowd pleaser.

And, no, Cuvée Rosé is not my favorite rosé Champagne. That's not because I think there is anything wrong with it. The truth is there is not a single thing wrong with this Champagne. Given the popularity of Cuvée Rosé, you could argue it is more likely there is something wrong with me. Or you could view this as a mere matter of preferences, as I do. Once you are able to appreciate the differences between reductive and oxidative Champagnes, you can see how these differences might—along with other factors—affect how much you enjoy a particular Champagne. For example, I take pleasure in Champagnes across a pretty wide spectrum of reductive and oxidative styles. But other factors come into play. I don't typically love very reductive rosés unless they have a lot of bottle age on them. However, if you pushed a glass of Cuvée Rosé my way at breakfast on a Sunday morning, or poolside on a scorching summer day, or at a time when I unexpectedly found myself in an unusually ebullient mood, I would go with it, probably enthusiastically. On the other side, many oxidative Champagnes strike me as perfect matches for food or contemplation, and some of these don't work as well for me as aperitifs in a crowd. Now, would I drink Krug Grand Cuvée if offered to me at any time of day, at any place, in any mood, with or without food, with or without contemplation? Let me think while I take one deep breath . . . sure.

Experimenting with reductive and oxidative Champagnes is a valuable process in the larger scheme of writing your own Champagne story, at least the one you'll tell today. Maybe you'll discover that you mostly prefer young, reductive Champagnes and that you find Krug Grand Cuvée too oxidative, no matter the occasion. Maybe you won't. And maybe you'll come to a different conclusion somewhere down the road. The possibilities are almost endless, and the story that matters is not the story of a Champagne style, or of a producer, or of a bottle of Champagne; it's yours. It's your taste. Grab a couple of bottles of Champagne, perhaps an apple, and start to discover it.

CHAPTER 5

Unleashing the Great Champagne Drinker Within You

Many years ago, I was casually acquainted with a man who was the editor-in-chief of one of the world's most popular food and entertaining magazines. That's a job that is pretty hard to leave at the office, as you're the guru in your social circle on topics of interest to just about everyone. One evening, he relayed an episode in which someone, earnestly in search of wisdom, asked him to share his "philosophy" of lighting cigars. "Can you believe that? *Philosophy*? I told this guy I take a lighter, hold the cigar, and set fire to it." To this gourmand, the simple pleasure of enjoying a cigar after dinner needed no philosophy, no deep layers of thought or emotion, no complicated processes, which might only interfere with the primal experience. And yet, I think the request wasn't as silly as it may sound; it was, in essence, about the quest to maximize joy.

A proper, dependable method for enjoying Champagne is this: grab the nearest cold bottle of Champagne, open it, pour some into an available clean glass, and drink it. If you do that, the chances are good the experience will not be terrible. And for many drinkers, that may be all they need to know or want to know about consuming Champagne.

For those who want to get the most joy out of drinking Champagne, however, there is more you should know, or at least consider. Part of the task actually involves forgetting or ignoring much of what is said about drinking Champagne that happens to be unreliable or stupid. Unless you've already spent a lot of time experimenting with Champagne and questioning old conventions and recent trends, the odds are you are not the best Champagne drinker you can be. Let's fix that.

Like the rest of the book, this chapter is written for you, the *individual* drinker. We won't all experience drinking Champagne in the same ways, and it's very unlikely any other person will always experience Champagne exactly as I do. Use this chapter not as a manual but as a guide to finding out what works best for you. To become a great Champagne drinker, you need to be able to know at any particular moment: (1) whether you should be drinking Champagne; (2) if it is time to drink Champagne, whether a specific bottle of Champagne is ready to be drunk; and (3) if it's time to drink Champagne and the bottle is ready to open, how to open and serve it. Don't worry—it's easy; maybe not as easy as torching a cigar, but easy.

Is It Time for Champagne?

Yes, it is. Drink Champagne whenever you feel like it. Seriously, if there is only one thing you take away from this book, I hope that is it. Okay, on to the next section.

Actually, there is a bit more to say about this, because the idea of drinking Champagne whenever the mood strikes doesn't resonate with very many people outside of France. Most of us have accepted three senseless cultural norms about drinking Champagne that, like other ideas that might have had a kernel of sensibility in prior generations but have been passed down without scrutiny into a society that doesn't need them, are difficult to shake. Let's shine a light on these bad ideas and see if we can't bury them for good.

Stupid Champagne Idea #1:
Champagne is only for celebrations

Only twice in my life have I been so outraged by a statement made in a periodical that I felt compelled to write a letter to the editor. I'm proud to say both of my letters were published, though my conceit is diminished somewhat by the fact that both letters were addressed to wine magazines. Anyway, *Decanter* magazine's Letter of the Month in the February 2017 issue was my argument that Champagne is not just for celebrations and can be enjoyed at any time. The problem is not that Champagne is poured at celebrations. The problem is that the link between Champagne and special occasions is so strong that many people evidently believe that if you are drinking Champagne you *must* be celebrating. The logical flipside is that if you aren't celebrating, you *shouldn't* be drinking Champagne. I order Champagne at a restaurant and am asked, "What are you celebrating?" I open Champagne at home, and a friend of a friend walks in and asks, "What's the occasion?" I want to say, "Look, man, nobody needs to be celebrating an anniversary or a promotion or a cheerful medical prognosis or anything to drink Champagne. It's okay to just like the product itself." But I usually respond with "I'm celebrating dinner," or "I'm celebrating 3:48 in the afternoon" and hope I've made the point.

Nobody knows for sure who or what was the original source of the Champagne/celebration meme. Maybe it goes all the way back to King Clovis, or maybe it derives from the coronation of later French kings in the Cathedral of Reims, and maybe it's a more recent idea. What is pretty clear is that the Champagne industry successfully jumped on the theme in 20th-century advertising. In any event, the idea that you shouldn't drink Champagne outside of a celebration is simply a consequence of culture. It doesn't have anything to do with a feature of the wine itself. It's not like saying, "Don't have coffee before bed" or "Don't drink tequila while piloting a commercial airliner."

If you really need to feel celebratory when drinking Champagne, then simply reverse the process and let Champagne bring the celebration to you instead of waiting for a celebration to bring Champagne. And if you feel like you need a special beverage to mark a special occasion, then buy a special bottle of Champagne. The point is: there is no good reason to deprive ourselves of Champagne merely because we aren't celebrating. Plus, there aren't enough tent-pole celebrations in life to explore the whole tapestry of Champagne. When you free yourself from the notion that there is something wrong with drinking Champagne outside of a celebration, you unlock more opportunities to experience what Champagne can deliver. Maybe you might even drink Champagne with meals. Wait—are you supposed to do that?

STUPID CHAMPAGNE IDEA #2:
CHAMPAGNE IS NOT FOR DRINKING WITH MEALS

Remember that time you were at a restaurant with a group of friends, and, once everyone had perused the dinner menu, the usual conversation broke out about what wine to order for the table, and someone said, "Well, this Champagne will pair beautifully with everything everyone is ordering," and the table agreed? Right. For at least 99% of the drinking population, that has never happened. Why? The reason people don't think Champagne is for pairing with meals may be a historical artifact—for a long time, sparkling wines from Champagne were mostly sweet wines that were considered a dessert. And now, in line with the celebration concept, Champagne is seen as a wine for raising a glass and making a toast before folks get to the serious business of eating a proper meal.

Once again, though, there is nothing about the qualities of Champagne that would make it inappropriate for pairing with a meal. Quite to the contrary, Champagne is one of the most versatile food wines we have. Its high acidity makes it perfect to pair with high-acid foods. Its texture and acidity balance rich and fatty foods. And light dosage and fruit flavors are a pleasurable contrast to salty foods. The wide range of Champagne styles—from oxidative, rich, fuller-bodied wines, to more-reductive, light, crisp wines—provides a variety of options for food pairings. And let's not forget, Champagne is made principally from two grapes—Chardonnay and Pinot Noir—that everyone seems to agree are perfect for food pairings when made into still wines. In my experience, the only foods that dry Champagnes don't pair well with are sweet desserts, including, oddly enough, wedding cake.

I think it's strange that people who are so willing to be adventurous about food, to try new dishes, new combinations of ingredients, and different ethnic cuisines, are afraid to try drinking Champagne with meals. Trust me, I frequently drink Champagne with meals, and there is nothing to fear. If you drink a few assorted Champagnes with a few different meals, you won't fracture the social order, you won't get arrested by the wine police, and you very likely will find pairings that work well for you. All you have to do is ignore two stupid Champagne ideas, or maybe three.

STUPID CHAMPAGNE IDEA #3:
CHAMPAGNE IS NOT FOR BREAKFAST

All right, that heading is a little ridiculous. But the point is that, except in unusual circumstances when a celebration demands drinking at a different time, Champagne is thought of as an aperitif to be served before dinner. We might call it the cocktail hour. There is something very time-bound about Champagne drinking. I'm not suggesting that you drink all day, only that there are situations in which groups of people find it appropriate to drink during different parts of the day, and Champagne is excluded from most of them for no good reason. Even brunch—which usually offers foods that pair extremely well with Champagne—customarily gets you the mimosa, an infantile beverage that truly should only be made with Prosecco.

I think the best temporal argument could be made for not drinking Champagne late at night, given that most Champagnes have delicate flavors that will be harder to detect as the day goes on. On the other hand, sometimes, you don't care. Waking up in the morning next to an empty bottle of Champagne bobbing in an ice bucket is like eating leftover birthday cake for breakfast; it's a libertine moment with few consequences. Besides, at little more than one-quarter of the alcohol by volume of most spirits, Champagne might be the smarter nighttime choice for plenty of drinkers I know.

I do have one suggestion as to when *not* to drink Champagne—obviously not including unsafe situations in which drinking is inappropriate. I don't drink Champagne when I'm in a bad mood or in any sort of quarrel. These disruptions make it much more difficult to appreciate subtle aromas and flavors, and, instead of lifting the mood, Champagne falls flat. When the wine's been drunk, you feel worse than before, and you've lost a bottle of Champagne. It's a double whammy. If you want bubbles when you're upset, grab sparkling water instead.

Bad moods and fights aside, you're cheating yourself if you continue to adhere to nonsensical limitations on the enjoyment of Champagne. So don't.

Drink or Hold?

If you've decided you are ready to open a bottle of Champagne—and I think we've settled that you are—the next question is whether the bottle is ready for you. In other words, if you were to grab the nearest bottle of Champagne and open it, would the wine have completed whatever development was necessary to be in prime drinking condition, or should you hold on to it for a while to allow it to mature?

Happily, it is very rare to find a Champagne that is not ready to drink in the way that an underripe peach would be unsatisfying to eat. The overwhelming majority of Champagne actually is designed for drinking as soon as you bring your bottle home from the store. Almost all non-vintage Champagnes are created in anticipation that they will not be aged extensively by the consumer. You can age these wines if you want, but the potential benefits of waiting three or more years to open most non-vintage Champagnes probably are outweighed by the risks of losing their characteristic freshness. Even at the other end of the spectrum, expensive vintage Champagnes that connoisseurs would argue need five, ten, or even more years of cellaring before they hit their peak, will be very satisfying to all but the most discerning Champagne drinkers upon release. So, my first piece of advice is to open whatever Champagne bottle you can get your hands on, without worrying very much about the bottle's age.

With that said, one of the fascinating ways of exploring Champagne—and another method of fine-tuning your preferences—is to experiment along the dimension of time. Like other wines, Champagne does develop in bottle. Whether those developments are positive or not is, for the most part, yet another subjective experience. If you want to go down this path of discovery—and I highly recommend it—the first thing you need to know is the age of your bottle of Champagne. When was the bottle born, so to speak? With most still wines, it's usually very easy to find out—just look at the vintage stated on the front label. However, in Champagne, the matter is much more complicated.

It is widely agreed that the "born on" date for Champagne is the date of disgorgement, when the dead yeast cells are removed, dosage is added, and the cork is inserted into the bottle. That's because the development of Champagne is very different before and after that date. Aging before disgorgement is characterized by autolysis, which not only develops yeasty aromas and flavors but also protects Champagne from oxidation and maintains its freshness. After disgorgement, a host of different reactions take place within the wine, caused by the introduction of sugar, contact with small amounts of oxygen through the cork, and other chemical reactions in the wine that will change a Champagne's flavor profile over time. Champagne producers typically disgorge even their vintage Champagnes several different times—sometimes separated by years—for reasons that include inventory control. That means, for example, that a particular 2008 vintage Champagne you buy from one retailer could be a materially different wine from the same Champagne sitting on a retail shelf somewhere else at the same time.

Given the importance of disgorgement dates to consumers, you might assume that every bottle of Champagne displays the date of its disgorgement in clear type on the back label. It doesn't sound so difficult, does it? A Champagne producer knows when every bottle was disgorged, has a label to affix to the bottle, and has the ability to put the date on that label. Bruno Paillard has been printing disgorgement dates on Champagne labels since 1983, and today many producers, both large and small, label their Champagnes with either the date, month, or quarter of disgorgement, or with a bottle code that can be typed or scanned to find the information online.

Unfortunately, many other producers refuse to disclose disgorgement dates. Their primary justification is a concern that consumers will not understand the significance of a disgorgement date and will confuse it with the "sell by" or "best by" dates commonly seen on perishable foods or the "born on" dates on some beers. They don't want you to interpret a disgorgement date from a year ago as a sign that the Champagne has gone bad. While I understand the concern in theory, it's pretty well established by now that Champagne consumers don't avoid Champagnes that bear disgorgement dates. And the easy way to avoid any possibility of a problem is to provide a code, as Krug and Roederer do, which allows a producer to give the disgorgement date on its website, where it can provide whatever context it thinks the consumer needs. I like knowing when my Champagne was disgorged, because I prefer to drink Champagne at least eighteen months after disgorgement and usually longer. And I want to taste Champagnes at different ages to experience how they have developed. It kills me to pay good money for Champagne that is not labeled with a disgorgement date or code. Hopefully, those producers who currently lack sufficient courage or interest in transparency eventually will get with the program. It seems like it should be one of the easier wine problems to solve.

Let's assume, though, that your Champagne bottle indicates it was disgorged a year ago. What can you expect if you open the bottle now compared to what would happen if you opened the bottle ten years from now? While it would be convenient to provide a chart of some type that lists the particular flavors to be found in Champagne over different periods of aging—and you can find these online—the truth is that there are too many variables to make specific predictions for any particular Champagne. In general, young Champagnes likely will emphasize fresh floral and fruit aromas and flavors, while older Champagnes will evolve to dried fruits and other characteristics that may be described as roasted, toasted, or candied. But as I've said in other parts of the book, to isolate one factor—in this case, the age of a Champagne—is not as interesting or relevant as experiencing how the factor plays out in a particular Champagne or a type of Champagne. For example, I happen to enjoy older vintage rosé Champagnes, sometimes more than twenty years old. They don't always hold up, but when they do, I'm bowled over at times by flavors of desiccated red fruit, tea, honey, and light oxidative aromas that only hint at what the wine was in its bright youth. But that still makes it almost impossible for me to say with confidence what I will find the next time I open another bottle of Champagne that has aged for the same length of time. While it's fine to have high-level ideas about how different types and styles of Champagne will evolve over the course of bottle aging, the ideas themselves lack importance. Drink and experience bottle age in Champagnes, then approach the next one you pour with an open mind.

There is another reason you really want to know the disgorgement date if you plan to drink a Champagne at an advanced age. Something else is aging along with the wine: the cork. Champagne corks are wider than the diameter of the bottle neck, and they are compressed before being inserted. When you remove a cork from a young Champagne, you may notice that the bottom of the cork immediately flares out to a diameter that is wider than the neck. But in an older bottle, the bottom of the removed cork might look more like a straight peg. That's because the pressure inside the bottle caused enough mechanical fatigue that the cork has lost some of its ability to spring back. Eventually, this could lead to a cork that practically glides out of a Champagne bottle—a terribly distressing sign that the wine most likely is ruined. Corks naturally allow a small amount of oxygen into the wine from the atmosphere and allow small amounts of carbon dioxide to escape, but a degraded cork will result in a Champagne that is badly oxidized and has few or no bubbles. There is no fixed term of a Champagne cork's life, and you can't do anything to reliably examine the cork without opening the bottle. Over time, I have developed a personal, unscientific rule of thumb: I almost always open my bottles of Champagne no more than twenty years after disgorgement. After twenty years, there is a greater risk than I want to accept that the Champagne will be spoiled. And much worse than not having any Champagne is having Champagne in your glass that you bought, stored, anticipated, and at some unknown point destroyed by storing too long.

To summarize: drink Champagne young, drink it in its midlife, and, before it dies, drink it old. And if the Champagne is dead, my other rule is to open another bottle as soon as possible to erase the memory.

Opening and Serving Champagne

It's remarkable how often you find that experimenting with all sorts of unconventional, complex, modern ways of doing something only takes you back to the beginning, to the power of the common, simple, old methods. This is what I have found with methods for opening and serving Champagne. In short, make it cold, keep it bubbly, and serve it in a wine glass. I'll tell you why and how.

The best place to start when thinking about opening and serving is the end: what do we want from Champagne when we drink it? For most of us, the answer is we want a refreshing, sparkling, cold wine that is recognizable as Champagne. Drink a glass of Champagne that has few bubbles, or Champagne that is just barely cool, or both, and see if you enjoy it as much. I'm guessing you won't. The reason is not merely that a preference for bubbly, cold Champagne seems fairly universal. It's because Champagne is *designed* to be drunk this way. It's assembled with the expectation that you will drink it bubbly and cold. If you don't, the Champagne you drink very likely will be out of balance or suboptimal in one or more ways.

Bubbles contribute to the drinking experience even while in the glass, sending aromas toward your nose as they burst on the surface of the wine. But most importantly, carbon dioxide is converted into carbonic acid in the mouth, which creates a tactile sensation on the tongue that feels like tingling and helps make Champagne refreshing and not cloying. Without bubbles, Champagne becomes an inharmonious still wine, just as Coke tastes terrible when it's flat. Serving Champagne cold also contributes to Champagne's vibrant character and its overall balance. We experience sweetness more intensely when we consume beverages served at higher temperatures. The subtle sweetness contributed by modest dosage in most Champagnes, intended to balance acidity, is perceived as elevated and out of balance when Champagne is not cold. While I am sure there are some whose preferences lie outside the norm, Champagne that is neither bubbly nor cold likely will be experienced by most of us as unbalanced, uninteresting, and unappetizing. This is why the two most important considerations in opening and serving are to keep Champagne cold and to preserve as much dissolved carbon dioxide in the wine as possible until the moment a glass is full of Champagne.

The first step in serving Champagne, therefore, is to chill the bottle to approximately 40°F. Chilling the bottle does more than make the wine cold; the colder the bottle is when the cork is popped, the more carbon dioxide will remain inside the wine instead of escaping through the neck of the bottle. To chill Champagne, first place the bottle in a large, empty bucket. Fill the bucket with ice, and then pour in cold water to the brim. Ice water, not ice alone, chills the bottle evenly and efficiently. Depending on the bottle's temperature before it began its ice bath, it should be ready to open in approximately fifteen to thirty minutes. This will allow you to serve Champagne in a glass at an initial temperature of around 45°F.

There is one best way to open a bottle of Champagne that is safe, preserves as much carbon dioxide as possible, and doesn't make you look like an idiot. First, remove the foil from the top and neck of the bottle. Usually this is as easy as pulling a tab, but sometimes there is no tab, and you may need a knife. The remaining instructions assume you are right-handed.

Start with the bottle standing on a table directly in front of you, with the wire tab of the *muselet* to your right. With your left hand, grasp the neck of the bottle by wrapping your fingers around it, and place your thumb over the top of the cork. From here on out, your left thumb will stay on top of the cork. Lift the bottle one-handed off of the table, and tilt the neck forward, so that the bottle is at a 45-degree angle to your body. With your right hand, pull down on the *muselet* tab and turn it toward you (counter-clockwise) six half-turns. This will loosen the *muselet* and open the tab completely. With your right thumb, push the *muselet* tab up against the side of the bottle neck.

Next, grab the base of the bottle with your right hand facing up, so that your other fingers are wrapped around the back of the bottle.

At this point, you may need to slide the fingers of your left hand up slightly, so that your index and middle finger are wrapped around the cork instead of the neck. Keeping your left hand stationary, slowly turn the base of the bottle counter-clockwise with your right hand. This action will loosen the cork. As you feel the cork start to eject from the bottle under pressure, apply a slight counter force on the cork with your left thumb. When the cork is about halfway out, push the cork slightly to the right side with your left thumb. What you should hear is a soft *pfffft* sound as the cork slowly leaves the bottle. You have now expertly opened a bottle of Champagne. Time to pour!

Before you pour, though, should you decant Champagne? Decanting Champagne has become popular in some circles. I won't burden you with my entire brief against it. I see absolutely no benefit to decanting Champagne. What decanting will do is transfer a significant amount of carbon dioxide into the atmosphere, making the Champagne that finally makes its way to your glass less bubbly. I can't decide whether decanting Champagne is sadistic, masochistic, or both; but in any case, I don't get it at all.

One other task before pouring is to find an appropriate wine glass. You want a glass whose shape allows you to smell the wine and facilitates a slow release of carbon dioxide. Strangely enough, the two most popular Champagne glasses—the flute and the coupe—do not meet both requirements. The flute's narrow opening makes it almost impossible to appreciate aromas in the glass. The coupe, on the other hand, creates a large surface area of wine and essentially generates a graveyard for bubbles. Flutes and coupes were designed with attractiveness in mind, not maximizing the pleasure of drinking Champagne. I refuse to drink Champagne out of either glass.

The good news is that you, your friends, and your favorite restaurants already have a glass that is perfectly suitable for Champagne: the standard medium-sized wine glass. In this glass, you can smell your

Champagne, and bubbles will be preserved well enough to make their way into your mouth. It's a simple solution, and it works. There is one other specialty glass that I prefer, but you really don't need it. It's a tulip-shaped Champagne glass, made by glassmakers such as Lehmann and Riedel, that is designed to allow bubbles to gradually reach the surface and then burst within a tapered top that briefly contains the wine's aromas. I drink Champagne from tulip-shaped glasses at home, but I repeat that you don't need them to enjoy Champagne. What you need is a proper glass—which could be a simple wine glass—that you use consistently when you drink Champagne. Whatever you do, don't overthink it.

A note about pouring: here too, dissolved carbon dioxide is at risk. The conventional way of pouring wine—straight down the middle of the glass—is not ideal for Champagne. Pouring Champagne into the middle of an empty glass results in a large head of froth and the premature release of carbon dioxide. To prevent this, pour carefully down the side of the glass instead. For the same reason of carbon dioxide preservation, don't swirl Champagne. Bubbles bursting at the surface do much of the work that swirling does for still wines, and it's just not worth it.

There is a lot more I could say about opening, serving, and drinking Champagne. But I wonder sometimes if today we rely too heavily on too many instructions, too many rules, too many experts, for tasks that don't genuinely require them. And I wonder if this doesn't lead to fewer personal, independent investigations, experiments, and explorations, and their intrinsic delights. I have provided you with what I believe is the basic information you should know if you want to drink Champagne well. As for the rest, I hope you will use your curiosity, your intuition, and your experience to find your own joy in what really is part of the fun of drinking Champagne. Oh, and buy magnums of Champagne. That's it.

CHAPTER 6

Drinking, Part 3: A Question of Place

Our final perspective is to look at Champagne not as a single wine region but as a collection of smaller places. In each place, grapes grow differently than they do in other parts of Champagne, and wines are produced that reflect the differences. It's endlessly fascinating and rewarding to drink wines from distinct winegrowing areas within Champagne, to find patterns, and once again to find your own preferences. In this chapter, I will start you on your way by providing a brief look at the four main subregions in Champagne. But before we get to that, it's important to gain a bit of perspective and clarity on two issues.

The first is this: Champagnes made exclusively from grapes grown in smaller areas within the Champagne region—subregions, villages, vineyards, parcels—are not necessarily better than Champagnes blended from grapes drawn from the four corners of this large wine region. In contrast to most other high-quality wine regions, such as Bordeaux and Burgundy, Champagne is first and foremost a wine made from the region as a whole. The overwhelming majority of Champagnes are blends from multiple subregions, villages, and vineyards, including many of the greatest wines produced in Champagne—Krug Grand

Cuvée, Louis Roederer Cristal, and Dom Pérignon, for example. This is not some quirk or flaw in Champagne but rather a feature. As I will explain below, the three Champagne grapes grow differently in different subregions. For this reason, producers who want to make the superior blends of Pinot Noir and Chardonnay, for example, typically will take Pinot Noir from the Montagne de Reims and Chardonnay from the Côte des Blancs, because that is where those grapes usually grow best. For those producers who are willing to pay for the best grapes to utilize for this type of blend, it would make no sense to limit themselves to a single village or subregion.

Champagnes labeled with a single village or a single vineyard did not exist in the marketplace a hundred years ago and, to this day, showcase differences in character more than differences in quality. Many of these wines are excellent and intriguing; however, poorly made single-village and even single-vineyard Champagnes are not hard to find. Although we have been trained to think otherwise by practices in other popular wine regions, narrowing the selection of grapes for a bottle of wine to a smaller area of vineyard land, by itself, does not necessarily increase a wine's quality.

For whatever reason, we are living in an age in which ever-smaller areas of vineyard land are glorified merely because they are small or smaller. This bias is similar to the misguided orientation toward grower Champagne, except in this case the object of fetish is not the wine-maker—or not only the winemaker—but a piece of land or a few pieces of land that most drinkers know nothing about. There is, particularly, something about the word *single* that drives many drinkers to lose all perspective. To step adjacent to wine for a moment, legions of whisky drinkers seem to "know" that Single Malt Scotch Whisky is, by defini-tion, superior to Blended Malt Scotch Whisky and to Blended Scotch Whisky, though I would bet that a healthy percentage of those who hold this belief could not explain what these labels mean, let alone defend the proposition. I mention all of this because it is very easy for a Champagne consumer to be misled by a village or vineyard designation on a label into thinking that the designation means something more than it does. And this is especially true when it comes to the unfortunate use of the terms Grand Cru and Premier Cru in Champagne.

The French terms Grand Cru and Premier Cru typically are translated into English as "great growth" and "first growth," where "growth" usually (but not always) refers to a specific and highly regarded area of land for growing wine grapes, typically a vineyard. However, there is no uniform system in France for classifying vineyards, wine producers, or wines as Grand Cru or Premier Cru, and several French wine regions do not use these terms at all. When a bottle of French wine is labeled with one of these terms, it is understandable for a consumer to assume that the designation means the wine is a very good (Premier Cru) or outstanding (Grand Cru). And if a label contains neither term, then perhaps the wine is of lesser quality. However, if the bottle of wine in question is Champagne, these assumptions are not correct.

The use of the terms Grand Cru and Premier Cru in Champagne is rooted in a system established in 1911 among grape growers and Champagne producers to set prices for grapes. Known as the *échelle des crus* ("ladder of growths"), this arrangement made it fairly simple to agree on grape prices each year. Eleven villages were considered Grand Cru, and prices of grapes grown in these villages were set at 100% of an agreed amount that producers would pay for a kilogram of grapes. Every other village was assigned a lower percentage, based on the perceived quality of grapes grown in that village, and the prices for grapes grown in each village were priced accordingly. Villages rated 90-99% were considered Premier Cru, and villages rated lower than 90% were simply referred to as *autre* ("other") crus. The Grand Cru and Premier Cru designations, therefore, were solely a means of lowering the annual transaction costs involved in the sale of grapes. And the *échelle des crus* as a whole was a series of convenient generalizations—villages contain many vineyards that diverge in quality, and some vineyards in Grand Cru villages are inferior to certain vineyards in Premier Cru villages. But most importantly for our purposes, the *échelle des crus* had nothing to do with rating finished Champagnes. It would have been as obvious in 1911 as it is now that poor Champagne can be made from grapes grown in Grand Cru villages.

In the late 20th century, the price-fixing feature of the *échelle des crus* was abandoned in favor of market prices set by individual agreements between producers and growers. Today, French wine law does not classify vineyards or wines in Champagne, as it does in Burgundy and Bordeaux. So why are some bottles of Champagne labeled Grand Cru or Premier Cru? Because French law permits it as an ill-fitting relic of the retired system. Any Champagne made entirely from grapes harvested from one or more of the seventeen Grand Cru villages or one or more of forty-two Premier Cru villages (as they were rated as of the date the system collapsed) may be labeled Grand Cru or Premier Cru, respectively. A Champagne made entirely from grapes grown in one Grand Cru village or one Premier Cru village may be labeled with the honorific designation in addition to the name of the village.

For the Champagne consumer, the important takeaways are that, first, the absence of the words Grand Cru or Premier Cru on a Champagne label does not indicate that the wine is inferior in any way. Cristal cannot be labeled Grand Cru because grapes from one Premier Cru village rated at 99% are blended into the wine, and Louis Roederer chooses not to label Cristal as Premier Cru. Other outstanding wines discussed earlier, such as Champagnes from Bérêche, Marie-Courtin, Moussé Fils, Tarlant, Ulysse Collin, and Vouette et Sorbée, are made entirely of grapes from villages that were ranked below Premier Cru. On the flip side, the fact that a Champagne is labeled Grand Cru or Premier Cru tells you something about the source of the grapes but tells you nothing about how carefully the grapes were tended or how skillfully the wine was made. Villages do matter in Champagne, but, for the drinker, the combination of skill and care in grape-growing practices and Champagne production matter more.

With those observations and clarifications out of the way, let's look at wines made in each of the four principal vineyard areas in Champagne: the Vallée de la Marne, the Montagne de Reims, the Côte des Blancs, and the Côte des Bar.*

Vallée de la Marne

It's easy to see on a map why the Vallée de la Marne is considered a distinct wine subregion—it's one long valley carved by the Marne River as it heads west through Champagne in the direction of Paris, with vines on both banks of the river. But for the Champagne drinker, it's better to think of the Vallée de la Marne as having two distinct parts.

The largest section, all but the most eastern ten percent, is home to Pinot Meunier. Pinot Noir and Chardonnay are grown here too, but they are in the minority because the western river valley can be very cool, foggy, and prone to spring frosts, leading to disease and destruction. It's the most challenging viticultural area in a challenging wine region. Pinot Meunier's somewhat shorter cycle from budding to ripening and its hardiness against cold weather make it a more natural fit than Pinot Noir or Chardonnay in most of the Vallée de la Marne. There are no Grand Cru or Premier Cru villages in this part of the valley, undoubtedly a reflection of the historical view of Pinot Meunier as Champagne's least impressive grape.

---

* The map in this book shows a fifth subregion, the Côte de Sézanne, which some consider to be part of the environs of the Côte des Blancs instead of a separate subregion. Although this part of Champange is interesting to explore, most of the grapes grown here are sold to the Champagne houses for blending with grapes from other subregions. We did encounter one Champagne produced here in Chapter 2, Ulysse Collin Les Maillons Blanc de Noirs.

And yet, as we have seen, conscientious growers have learned to cultivate Pinot Meunier that doesn't merely survive but thrives. Producers—usually the same people as the growers—have devoted themselves to putting Pinot Meunier in a leading role and making it shine. In Chapter 2, I discussed two 100% Pinot Meunier Champagnes from the Vallée de la Marne: Moussé Fils Special Club and Bérêche et Fils Rive Gauche. If you look back at my descriptions, you might notice distinctions that reflect the positions of two villages on opposite sides of the Marne River. The vineyards of Moussé Fils are located in Cuisles, on the right bank, where southern exposure to the sun promotes ripe fruit and rich, full-bodied wines. Bérêche's wine is made from grapes grown on the other side of the river, where northern exposure leads to greater freshness, more restraint, and elegance. This is only one example of the interesting contrasts and patterns in the larger stretch of the Vallée de la Marne. Françoise Bedel and Tarlant, growers discussed earlier in this book, epitomize the spirit of pioneers in the Vallée de la Marne and produce Champagnes that are as enthralling as they are delicious. To truly explore the Champagnes of the greater portion of the Vallée de la Marne is to drop all preconceptions and simply drop in.

What I have not discussed much thus far is the other part of the Vallée de la Marne, the handful of villages in the valley's eastern edge. This small area is no less than the historical and present-day heart of Champagne. Sometimes called the Grande Vallée de la Marne, this slice of the valley is warmer, with vineyards situated on the right bank, exposed to the south, and planted mostly to Pinot Noir. This is a winegrowing area older than a millennium, which played a large role in making Champagne's reputation long before Champagne was sparkling. It is the home of the Abbey of Hautvillers, whose vineyards famously were tended by Dom Pierre Pérignon. And it holds the commune of Épernay, the commercial center of Champagne, where titanic houses—those of Moët & Chandon, Pol Roger, and Mercier, for example—line the

Avenue de Champagne. This smaller segment of the Vallée de la Marne deserves the label "Grand."

In Chapter 2, I discussed one Champagne made in the Grande Vallée de la Marne. Geoffroy Rosé de Saignée is produced from grapes grown in the Premier Cru village of Cumières, which marks the western end of his area. It's a splendid illustration of Champagne from the Grande Vallée de la Marne, where Pinot Noir is grown to a high degree of ripeness, and Champagnes are powerful and expressive. Let's look further now, by examining two Champagnes from the heart of the heart.

Gatinois Brut Réserve

Sometimes when you narrow the focus of your attention to a specific place, a small place, you facilitate a connection with history. This is why we visit historical sites: not to gaze upon a physical object or structure, but to employ the place as a portal to commune with human beings who were there before us and, in that way, more fully comprehend our own humanity. It cannot be denied that this is accessible through wine. In the right circumstances, wine is a looking glass into the past. This is not about drinking wine that tastes the way it did many centuries ago—you should hope it doesn't. Rather, when drinking wine made from grapes grown in an old wine village of historical importance, it may be possible for the thoughtful and the sensitive to follow a thread back in time and, by doing so, to join the past.

There is no village in Champagne of greater historical importance than Aÿ, the sole Grand Cru in the Vallée de la Marne. From our vantage point today, we look at a village such as Aÿ and say it is a part of Champagne, as an arm is a part of a person. But it's more accurate to say that Champagne came out of Aÿ and a few other nearby villages that earned individual renown for their wines. Popes, kings, and poets of the middle ages celebrated the still wines of Aÿ, making Aÿ famous as the source of exceptional wines long before Champagne earned its reputation as a winemaking region.

Today, the village's tradition is carried forward by growers like the Gatinois family, whose lineage can be traced back to 17th-century grape growers in Aÿ. The Brut Réserve is quintessential Aÿ Champagne and a link to the past. A blend of 80% Pinot Noir and 20% Chardonnay, ripe fruit, especially red fruit, is front and center in a full-bodied Champagne that tilts away from freshness in the direction of boldness and vigor. The term "full-bodied" is used incorrectly far too often when describing Champagne. With moderate alcohol, high acidity, and subtle flavors, Champagne only rarely conveys the impression of weight on the palate that would justify this label. If you want to know what full-bodied really is in Champagne, drink Gatinois Brut Réserve.

It's this quality in Gatinois's Champagne that provides a conduit to feel yourself joined with history. The Brut Réserve is a sparkling wine that drinks like smooth, dense, mouth-coating still wine that happens to have bubbles. It's less a modern Champagne for modern drinking than a nectar. Almost inconceivable as an aperitif in casual company, it drinks like wine for a royal banquet. It is possible to peek, in this way, at the great still wines of Aÿ of long ago, at Champagne before it was Champagne, and at wines made by long-forgotten grape growers and winemakers and enjoyed by long-remembered popes, kings, and poets. There is no history in glasses of wine, but in some there are signals waiting to be heard. From the village of Aÿ, the signals are in Gatinois Brut Réserve.

PHILIPPONNAT CLOS DES GOISSES

Aÿ's neighbor to the east is Mareuil-sur-Aÿ. While Aÿ was rated 100% in every iteration of the *échelle des crus*, Mareuil-sur-Aÿ was rated 90% in 1911, leaped to 95% in 1920, and finally made it to 99% in 1985, where it remains in perpetuity as one of the two villages that are short of Grand Cru status by one percent. The notion that grapes from every vineyard in Mareuil-sur-Aÿ are worth exactly one percent less than those of every vineyard next door in Aÿ points to the absurdity of the *échelle des crus*, a system constructed by politics much more than reason and fossilized on labels much more likely to mislead than inform. It's one illustration out of many that suggests taking Grand Cru and Premier Cru designations with a grain of salt.

In any event, it's hard to feel too sorry for Mareuil-sur-Aÿ. Because while the village does not have and will never have a Grand Cru ranking, it does have the Champagne house of Philipponnat, established there in 1910 by a family that traces its roots to grape growers in Aÿ as far back as 1522. And it has one of the most esteemed vineyards in all of Champagne, from which is made an extraordinary single-vineyard Champagne of the same name: Clos de Goisses.

The Clos de Goisses vineyard is distinguished by its warmth.* It lies on a slope that is unusually steep for Champagne—in some parts, the angle of the slope is forty-five degrees. It also has the advantage of facing due south, directly in front of the Marne Canal. The consequence is that vines are bathed in sunlight all day long, and grapes ripen more quickly and can be harvested at greater levels of maturity than grapes in nearby vineyards. There is another dimension at play as well. A single-vineyard Champagne tends to conjure an image of a small vineyard, typically planted to one grape variety, and used almost exclusively to make one or more single-vineyard wines. But the Clos de Goisses vineyard is more like Philipponnat's palette. At more than thirteen acres of

---

* A *clos* is an enclosed vineyard, generally surrounded by a wall tall enough to produce a warm microclimate. There are around thirty recognized *clos* in Champagne, though fewer than half as many are used to bottle single-vineyard Champagnes in significant quantities. This being Champagne, where exactitude apparently is optional, it is unsurprising that Clos de Goisses—which was called simply Les Goisses until 1956—technically is not a *clos* because it is not enclosed by a wall (it has a retaining wall at the bottom of the slope). But because the vineyard does have a warm microclimate, as would be expected of a *clos*, because Clos des Goisses was the very first single-vineyard Champagne and is one of the great Champagnes available today, and because Mareuil-sur-Aÿ got ripped off in the *échelle des crus*, I suggest the Champagne drinker look the other way in this instance.

Pinot Noir and Chardonnay, divided into fourteen parcels, it is large for a vineyard in Champagne that has only one owner and is used for a single-vineyard wine. This gives Philipponnat the opportunity to select the finest material each year, given the conditions of each vintage, to blend into Clos de Goisses. In fact, it is rare for all fourteen parcels to make it into the Clos de Goisses in any one year. In some years, fewer than half are employed for that purpose. The Champagne usually is a blend of about 65% Pinot Noir and 35% Chardonnay, but this can vary.

The upshot is that the essential character of Clos des Goisses is not found in a predictable flavor profile that can be teased out of the glass reliably each year. Rather, the hallmark of Clos des Goisses is not *what* it expresses but *how* it expresses. Clos des Goisses is first about power and, second, restraint. It's this tension between pushing and pulling in harmony that so often makes a great wine. "Powerful"—like "full-bodied"—is a term used too liberally to describe Champagnes. Most Champagnes are not, and should not be, powerful. A powerful Champagne is uncommonly flavorful, demonstrating in your mouth the potency of exceptionally ripe fruit. A powerful Champagne is uncommonly long, carrying those flavors through a finish that continues after the point of mere satisfaction. And a powerful Champagne is unusually covetous of your physical and mental attention, moving you to stand up straight if you are slouching in the least. The most powerful Champagne discussed in this book is, undoubtedly, Clos des Goisses. And yet Clos des Goisses would not qualify as great if it were merely powerful. Restraint in wine curbs power for the sake of harmony. Philipponnat blocks malolactic conversion in Clos des Goisses, which, along with the blending of Chardonnay, assures refreshing acidity and a vibrant, zesty mouthfeel that are necessary in a wine this immense.

As you might expect, Clos des Goisses is widely considered to be a gastronomic Champagne, and Philipponnat markets it as such. I don't disagree. But personally, I enjoy Clos des Goisses without food, as a spectacle. I don't want to lose sight of the wonders of this wine in a forest of a meal, to shade the effects or blunt the impact. There are Champagnes to which you give attention, and then there is Clos des Goisses, to which you give heed.

Montagne de Reims

There essentially are two stories to be told about the subregion known as the Montagne de Reims, one simple and one not.

The simple, most common story reflects the reality that if your neighborhood wine shop carries a few single-village Champagnes from this subregion, the chances are good that they will all come from only two neighboring Grand Cru villages—Ambonnay and Bouzy. That is understandable, because these are the two most famous, most highly regarded villages from the Montagne de Reims, and several high-quality producers from each village sell their single-village Champagnes internationally. When the Montagne de Reims is understood through the wines of Ambonnay and Bouzy, the story of the subregion is of bold, concentrated Champagnes dominated by Pinot Noir grown in warm vineyard sites on slopes facing south and southeast. If you tried either of the Ambonnay *blanc de noirs* from Egly-Ouriet or Paul Déthune, discussed in Chapter 2, you've tasted this narrative.

A less distorted, more complex story is that the Montagne de Reims is diverse in many ways. Vineyards are planted on slopes around a forested plateau, except on the western side. On a map, this gives the impression of vineyard areas laid out in a shape that looks something like a horseshoe. Thus, while Ambonnay and Bouzy are on the south side of the mountain, other villages are situated around the plateau to the east, north, and northwest. The consequence is that grapes grown in villages around the horseshoe can ripen differently, and there is no one best grape variety for the entire subregion. Collectively, Ambonnay and Bouzy are planted to about 85% Pinot Noir, but Pinot Noir represents only a plurality of plantings in the Montagne de Reims, with Chardonnay and Pinot Meunier representing about 60% of the grapes harvested in this subregion.

We already have seen in three Champagnes, how variable the Montagne de Reims can be beyond the southern side of the hill. Vilmart's vineyards are in Rilly-la-Montagne on the northern side of the plateau, where mostly north-facing slopes are conducive to growing all three grape varieties in an extended growing season that is traditional in Champagne. In Vilmart's Cuvée Rubis, the effects of location and aspect are found in a rosé that is brisk, juicy, and animated on the palate. Further to the northwest is the small village of Ormes, where Pinot Meunier is the dominant grape variety, but from which Bérêche draws on Pinot Noir and Chardonnay for its elegant, restrained Campania Remensis. Northwest of Reims is Merfy and the southwest-facing vineyard of Les Barres, which is the source of Chartogne-Taillet's mosaic *blanc de noirs*, consisting entirely of Pinot Meunier. And this really is just the beginning of what is possible. But while the possibilities for Champagne in the Montagne de Reims are endless, this book is not. Let's consider just two more Champagnes and what else they have to tell us about the Montagne de Reims.

FRÉDÉRIC SAVART L'OUVERTURE

It's fairly audacious to claim—as Frédéric Savart does on the front labels of his bottles of Champagne—to make singular, unique wines. For all we know, someone else down the road or in some other corner of Champagne could be making Champagnes very similar to Savart's. But from what I can tell, Savart's wines are unique, are distinctive. And I think they provide a valuable insight into the way of understanding Champagne.

In the northwestern portion of the Montagne de Reims is the Premier Cru village of Écueil. It is here that Frédéric Savart owns ten acres of vineyards—less than the Clos de Goisses—planted mostly to Pinot Noir, with some Chardonnay. L'Ouverture is Savart's entry-level Champagne, made 100% from Pinot Noir. It doesn't taste like other *blanc de noirs*. It isn't ample and rich like the Champagnes from Ambonnay. It doesn't accomplish a seamless transfer of the typical aromas and flavors of Pinot Noir in the way that the Ulysse Collin and Marie-Courtin *blanc de noirs* do. It's fruity in a less overt, aggressive manner; it's delicate, understated, and soft. And I think, most interestingly, what sets L'Ouverture apart is its surprising piquancy. To call it tart wouldn't be quite correct. The texture is more zesty, stimulating in the mouth in a very pleasurable way, rather than biting or sharp. L'Ouverture is a Champagne of beautiful simplicity and finesse, but also of energy and a certain tension. It's a Champagne that is compelling in its own way, not in the way one would expect.

Champagnes that are unusual and unexpected—even slightly so—expand our understanding of what is possible. If they also are quality wines, as L'Ouverture is, Champagnes that aren't easily categorized or abstracted are pure gold. They enlarge the reach not merely of what you know but of what you can enjoy. The difficulty is that so often we are blind to the uncommon qualities of these wines because we taste within a framework of assumptions. This is the danger not of learning facts and generalizations about wine but of accepting them as universal truths that control the process of exploring any particular wine. You're told that Pinot Noir expresses itself in Champagne in some number of recognizable ways. The Montagne de Reims produces Champagnes in some number of styles. And once you have expertly internalized it all, you start looking for one or more well-accepted answers in a glass and miss what is actually there. To really appreciate the Champagnes of Frédéric Savart—in this example, L'Ouverture—you must start from a different place. You need to be open to the possibility that a wine will surprise you. It's only when you relax the influence of what you already know about Champagne that you unlock your capacity to truly taste Champagne.

I mentioned that L'Ouverture is Frédéric Savart's entry-level Champagne, and you might wonder why I'm carrying on about a $50 wine in a range that gets much more expensive. I think it's a common error to ignore the possibilities in entry-level Champagnes. It's so tempting to look to the next wine up the ladder, and then to the next one, which would seem to possess greater potential to reveal something special. But unique, singular wines need not be very expensive. L'Ouverture wins first prize at being what it is. You only have to look.

A. MARGAINE LE BRUT PREMIER CRU

Another interesting feature of the Montagne de Reims is that, as the vineyard area curves around the mountain to the east, Chardonnay dominates in four villages collectively referred to as the *Perle Blanche* ("white pearl"). These villages—Villers-Marmery, Trépail, Billy-le-Grand, and Vaudemange—had once been planted mostly to Pinot Noir and were not highly acclaimed. But they underwent a transformation to predominantly Chardonnay vineyards in the second half of the twentieth century and were elevated to Premier Cru status in 1985. The advantage of growing Chardonnay in these villages is that their vineyards face east and southeast, capturing the morning sun without baking in sun all day long. This is a principal reason why Chardonnay thrives in the Côte des Blancs, which I will address next. Champagnes from the Perle Blanche can be very similar to those from the Côte des Blancs, and, once again, it is dangerous and unhelpful to make distinctions with certainty. Nevertheless, there are Champagnes from this area of the Montagne de Reims that can show distinctive characteristics.

In Villers-Marmery, well over 90% of the vineyard area is planted to Chardonnay, with small plantings of Pinot Noir. It is here that the grower A. Margaine produces a line of expressive Champagnes. And as is the case with Savart, we don't need to go beyond the entry-level Champagne, Le Brut, for a fine example. Le Brut is composed of 90% Chardonnay and 10% Pinot Noir, and the current release contains a generous 60% of reserve wines from six different vintages. The texture is very interesting, especially in comparison to other Chardonnay-dominant Champagnes. It's light and vibrant enough to be very refreshing, but it's also dense, plush, and voluptuous. The fruit is not about bright lemons and green apples, but concentrated aromas and flavors of oranges and apricots. There is a honeyed element to the Champagne, which fits with Le Brut's overall intense, rich character. And yet, it lacks the warmth of Champagnes made from Chardonnay grown on the south side of the Montagne de Reims.

I've emphasized texture and mouthfeel frequently in this book, because it seems to me that these elements of Champagne, unfortunately, are thought to be the realm of experts, not ordinary drinkers. Maybe it's universally easier, more accessible, to employ our vocabulary of aromas than it is to conceptualize and reduce to words the ways in which liquids feel in our mouths. And maybe this is why terms such as minerality, linear, angular, vertical, and such, when used by experts to describe wines, seem so abstruse to the average drinker; thus, the entire topic of texture feels unapproachable. But let's get back to basics with Champagne. Compared to most still wines, Champagne's aromas and flavors are more subtle, less forward, less prominent in their relationship with other components of the wine. On the other hand, compared to most still white wines (we will leave tannic red wines out of the discussion), Champagne's mouthfeel is a more prominent feature of the wine. So, use whatever words make sense to you when describing a Champagne's mouthfeel—use grunts if you need to. But whatever you do, pay close attention to this aspect of Champagne, at least as much as you do to aromas and flavors. This is how, over time, you will notice patterns, differences, and your preferences in Champagne.

Ending our discussion of the Montagne de Reims with Chardonnay feels like putting on a warm-up act before the main event. Because in Champagne, Chardonnay truly is king in only one place: the Côte des Blancs.

Côte des Blancs

In trying to understand the Côte des Blancs, we face a situation that is somewhat the opposite of the one presented by the Montagne de Reims. That is, there is a simple explanation of what the Côte des Blancs is, which happily is true. And there is another, much more complicated explanation that, if not flatly untrue, is at least misleading and unhelpful. Fortunately, the simple, true explanation is all you really need to explore the Côte des Blancs. And luckily enough too, there is a familiar way of cutting through the complex explanation so that it won't present any obstacles in your journey.

The simple account of the Côte des Blancs is that it is planted 97% to Chardonnay and is universally regarded as the source of the greatest Chardonnay in Champagne. Along a stretch of east-facing slopes descending from a ridge perpendicular to the Marne Valley are six contiguous Grand Cru villages as well as other highly regarded Chardonnay vineyards. Every large Champagne house sources Chardonnay for its top wines from the Côte des Blancs, typically from one or more Grand Cru villages. Take three of the Champagnes discussed in Chapter 2: Louis Roederer Blanc de Blancs (starting with the 2013 vintage) is made exclusively from Chardonnay grown in the Grand Cru village of Avize; Taittinger Comtes de Champagnes is labeled Grand Crus and is a blend of Chardonnay from five of the six Grand Cru villages; and the Chardonnay blended into Louis Roederer Cristal is sourced from four of the Grand Cru villages. With a few notable exceptions, the most highly regarded growers of Chardonnay and producers of estate *blanc de blancs* in Champagne are located in the Côte des Blancs, usually in Grand Cru villages. Examples mentioned in this book are Pierre Péters and Agrapart & Fils. To get to know the Côte des Blancs, you let loose and drink *blanc de blancs* from all over the place and see what you think. That's it.

Now, for the rather sizable *but*. But this simple instruction won't do, we're told by some wine experts, in a small region or subregion or a string of villages, where only one grape variety is grown in significant quantities. And look just to the south of Champagne in Burgundy. There it is orthodoxy that distinctions between two wines can be traced reliably (and blindly) to the harvesting of the same single grape variety for the two wines from two different villages, vineyards, or plots across the same slope. For that reason, the accepted notion is that you can't really appreciate Burgundy unless you understand and can recognize many of the already agreed-upon distinctions in glasses of wine. Why would it be any different in the Côte des Blancs? Once you accept that as a rhetorical question, you move on to attempt to learn about the supposed differences between Champagnes made from the adjacent Grand Cru villages, at the very least. And I believe that this is an unnecessary and largely fruitless exercise.

It is not that a grape variety can't express itself differently when grown in different vineyards. We know that it can and does. The issue is that the more a set of vineyards are very similar in terms of the relevant natural factors, such as aspect, altitude, soils, microclimates, disease pressures, etc., the more likely it is that any differences that might be expressed in wines could be obliterated by variations in viticultural and winemaking practices. This is one reason why, I believe, that if you survey the literature on Burgundy, you will see much general agreement (not perfect agreement) on the typical differences between wines made from Chardonnay grown in different renowned villages in the Côte de Beaune; variations in winemaking practices can be significant, but they do not result in an abundance of radically different wine styles (as opposed to wines of different of levels of quality).

Champagne is not comparable. In my unscientific analysis of what a dozen contemporary Champagne experts have said about the typical characteristics of Champagnes from the Grand Cru villages in the Côte des Blancs, I found much less consistency, much less clarity, and a dearth of justifications. Again, I am not suggesting that there are no discernible differences between these villages that could, with every other factor controlled, result in different Champagnes, even from adjoining Grand Cru villages. But that's the rub. In Champagne, choices in the vineyard—and especially in the cellar—make styles, as I have discussed throughout this book. If you have developed a sense of Champagne and compare a reductive and an oxidative Champagne from Avize, for example, I think you will be more focused on the differences between the wines than the similarities.

If you truly want to understand and appreciate anything, you'll inevitably need to make decisions about the relative importance of data. I've drawn lines in this book that I believe are sensible for the lover of Champagne, and this is one of them. On the other hand, if you set out to prove the existence of readily identifiable village signatures in Champagnes from the Côte des Blancs that transcend choices in the vineyard and the cellar, and you accomplish that task, I will think that is completely awesome. For the rest of us, the way forward in the Côte des Blancs is exactly at it is in every other aspect of Champagne: to explore a style or a place, drink Champagnes made by quality producers, enjoy, learn, and repeat. I've described several such Champagnes already, but let's look at two more.

Doyard Vendémiaire Blanc de Blancs

Let me expand briefly on the process I just mentioned—drink from quality producers, enjoy, learn, repeat—and give an example. The first part requires you to know of the existence of a quality producer. I've mentioned many in this book, but there are countless more I have left out. There are several books that provide long lists of producers with the writer's subjective ratings, and much of the same information can be found on the Internet. If you took some time to read about producers in the Côtes des Blancs from just about any source, for example, it wouldn't take long before you stumbled upon Doyard. From north to south, the final Grand Cru village in the Côte des Blancs is Le Mesnil-sur-Oger. And just south of that is Vertus, a village that received a score of 95%, and thus the designation Premier Cru, on the final *échelle des crus.* It is in Vertus that the Doyard family has been producing Champagne for almost a hundred years, though the family's experience as growers in Champagne stretches back to the 17th century. Doyard owns approximately twenty-five acres of vines, mostly Chardonnay spread out in the Côte des Blancs over Vertus and the Grand Cru villages of Avize, Cramant, Oger, Le Mesnil-sur-Oger, as well as some Pinot Noir in Aÿ. The family successfully sells and exports a line of Champagnes that consistently receive critical acclaim. On this record, you would reasonably conclude that the Doyards know a thing or two about growing grapes and producing Champagne in the Côte des Blancs.

When you learn of a producer like Doyard but haven't tried its Champagnes, and assuming you are sufficiently motivated, set out on a path of exploration that has two elements: discover whether you like the wines, and see if you can learn something—anything—from them. Great joy and learning often are to be found in a producer's basic, least expensive Champagne. I believe there is no better example of that than Doyard Vendémiaire. It's a wine I enjoy very much, a wine that has at least a few things to teach.

Let's start with how the Champagne tastes and work back to the details. The first whiff of Vendémiaire in the glass is the aroma of Chardonnay from the Côte des Blancs. It's what a candle called Essence of the Côte des Blancs—if ever there were such a candle—should smell like. It's a racy, uplifting mixture of lemons, apples, toast, slightly roasted and entirely inviting. On the palate, the underlying texture, which is most apparent on the finish, is the same fine-grained mouthfeel that is so prominent in the much more expensive Pierre Péters Champagne discussed in Chapter 2. This aspect of texture is part of an overall harmony of notes, from creamy richness and roundness, to zippy lightness and liveliness. In this way too, Vendémiaire perfectly represents the Côte des Blancs. It's mouthwatering, long, and delicious. As I write this, I'm drinking Vendémiaire, snacking on salted cashews, and thinking that life is pretty good right now.

What can we learn here? The first lesson you could learn from Vendémiaire is that, even in highly rated areas of the Côte des Blancs, wonderful Champagne that expresses the typicity of a place does not have to be expensive. Vendémiaire is classic Côte des Blancs Chardonnay, something you will recognize after you have tried a few examples, such as those discussed earlier in the book. It's a high-quality benchmark at a reasonable price point. Once you know that from your own experience, it's much easier to assess value and quality in other Champagnes from the Côtes des Blancs. This wine costs about $45, and personally, I'm going to insist that competing Champagnes in this price range deliver about the same level of quality.

Recognizing the typicity and quality of this Champagne raises another question: what caused it to be so good? To know the answer to that question opens the possibility of finding more high-value Champagnes. This question takes us to the heart of discussions in this book about the roles of people and places in Champagne. I've suggested that it's a mistake to get too caught up in either categories of people or sizable places. Great Champagne is not made by titles, whether the title is held by a person or a village. What Vendémiaire shows is that great Champagne is made by certain people, who make quality-determinative choices, and who use superior grapes, grown in the right places. Yes, one reason Vendémiaire is of such high quality is that it is made from Chardonnay grown in top vineyards in the Côte des Blancs. But mere location is just one element. Let's look at what the people—the Doyard family—do with this prime vineyard land to make Vendémiaire.

In the vineyard, they cultivate old vines that consistently have produced excellent grapes. They use organic and biodynamic farming methods, ensuring the ongoing health and vitality of their vineyards. They select fruit judiciously, ensuring that only the most worthy grapes make it to the press and also ensuring that they bottle and sell a lot less Champagne than they could. The cellar contains Champagne presses that are more modern and expensive than necessary, resulting in cleaner, finer juice. Here again, the amount of Champagne that could be produced is reduced by the Doyards' decision to use only a portion of the *cuvée* from the press for the estate's Champagnes. Grapes from each parcel are vinified separately, and a portion of the wine used to make Vendémiaire is aged in old Burgundy barrels. Once bottled, the wine is aged on its lees for around five years—a remarkably long period for a non-vintage wine at its low price point. When you consider what might have happened had Doyard not made all of these choices and executed them well, it's obvious that there is nothing inevitable about Champagne made from great vineyard sites.

Vendémiaire is excellent because vineyards in particular villages of the Côte des Blancs are perfectly situated for the growing of Chardonnay *and* because of the Doyards' effort, care, determination, skill, experience, and love of Champagne. Enjoy, learn, repeat.

Jacques Lassaigne Extra Brut Blanc de Blancs Le Cotet

Montgueux is nowhere near the Côte des Blancs. The village is about fifty miles south of Vertus and sticks out as an isolated island of Champagne vineyards surrounded by villages that are not authorized for the growing of Champagne grapes. It's a relatively new growing area in Champagne and had few vineyards prior to the 1960s. It was rated at the lowest possible percentage (80%) in the *échelle des crus*. So what is Montgueux doing in a section about the Côte des Blancs? Well, for one thing, there has been no consensus about how to categorize Montgueux, and one solution has been to call it part of the Côte des Blancs environs. I think that result is perfectly fine. Montgueux is planted 90% to Chardonnay and is an important source of this grape variety for large Champagne houses. The reputation of Montgueux as the source of outstanding Chardonnay is such that many years ago the *chef de cave* of a prestigious house called Montgueux the "Montrachet of Champagne." I include a Champagne from Montgueux here for those reasons and because it gives me an excuse to talk about the most famous grower-producer in Montgueux, Jacques Lassaigne, and a wonderful, glorious *blanc de blancs*, Le Cotet.

Le Cotet is a single-vineyard, non-vintage Champagne crafted by Emmanuel Lassaigne, the proprietor and winemaker of the estate that bears his father's name. Le Cotet is an outstanding example of a Champagne that tastes like white Burgundy with bubbles. Lassaigne's entry-level wine, Le Vignes de Montgueux, gives the same impression at perhaps a lesser depth. In both wines, an extended fermentation, malolactic conversion, bottling at a lower level of atmospheric pressure, and the lack of dosage contribute to a sense of vinosity, of drinking an expressive fusion of dry still and sparkling wine. Champagnes bottled with less than the standard amount of sugar at *tirage* tend to show a less assertive mousse, which I don't view as positive or negative in the abstract. The question is how that element contributes to the overall construction of a particular Champagne. Le Cotet is about putting Chardonnay on center stage and revealing the grape at its most grand. In this context, bubbles play their essential role—this is Champagne, after all—but they are toned down to harmonize with the wine's theme, its purpose.

Of course, a Champagne produced in this way—leaving Chardonnay naked, so to speak—will work only when made with exceptional fruit.

And this takes us back to the relative influences of land and human being, but this time with the person standing in the vineyard instead of the cellar. Let's grant that the parcel in the Le Cotet vineyard harvested for this wine is superior in its potential to produce high-quality Champagne. We would all agree that potential is only that; the actual quality of grapes harvested will depend on the practices and skill of the persons responsible for tending the vineyard. This work is performed out of sight of the wine drinker, and the matter is mostly reduced to a question of trust in a grower or producer. But there is one exception, one bit of information that could be useful or could be distracting, that does tend to reach consumers these days and that I have mentioned in this book: the growing of grapes organically or biodynamically.* It's rarely mentioned on Champagne labels, but Champagne producers and their sponsors are promoting the subject at an ever-increasing pace, and I expect labeling is just a wave or two away. For the Champagne drinker, the question is whether you should view organic or biodynamic grapes as an indication of quality in a bottle of Champagne. I believe the answer is, in general, yes. However, the details are in the reasoning. I'll offer you mine, and I encourage you to think through it yourself.

We have to start with the honest conclusion that there is no scientific proof—and there probably never will be—that grapes farmed organically or biodynamically will, compared to conventionally farmed grapes,

---

* There are no universally agreed definitions of organic or biodynamic viticulture. In general, organic viticulture seeks to improve the health of a vineyard and preserve its ecology for the future. Synthetic fertilizers, fungicides, pesticides, and herbicides—which cure disease at the expense of long-term health—are avoided. Cover crops, organic composts, tilling, the use of animals and plants, along with judicious use of copper and sulfur, are tools of organic viticulture. Biodynamic practices generally start with organic viticulture and add some number of soil preparations or cosmological practices that aim to achieve optimal health and balance. An example is Preparation 500, which involves burying a cow horn stuffed with manure in the winter and eventually diluting the manure with rainwater and spraying it onto the soil. While there are various certification organizations, the fact that a grower is not a member of one or another is not consequential. What matters are a grower's practices.

result in superior Champagne, holding all other elements of production constant. You would have to grow grapes in separate greenhouses to test the question, and if anyone ever conducted the experiment, my guess is that the proposition would fail. I'm aware of only one experiment of this kind that involved vegetables grown organically and conventionally, and the test consumers couldn't tell the difference. Champagne presents an even more challenging trial, because only the juice of the fruit is extracted, after which it is highly processed into a sparkling wine. As always, I'm willing to be surprised, but I'm not holding out hope on this front.

At least two studies have purported to show that organic wines are, on average, "better" than conventional wines. They rely on statistical analyses of professional wine ratings, and they claim that wine professionals tend to rate organic wines slightly higher than comparably priced, comparably made non-organic wines. These studies have been reported in the press as proving the point I said hasn't been proved, and they don't. There were no scientific controls that would allow anyone to isolate the effects of organic or biodynamic viticulture. Nobody knows, as to any particular wine, what the rating would have been if a single different choice had been made—either to farm grapes organically or conventionally—and if all else had remained constant. Nevertheless, I am not surprised by the results. In Champagne, only a small percentage of the vineyard area is farmed organically or biodynamically, due in large part to the difficulty of employing these practices in Champagne's cold, variable climate. But an outsized percentage of excellent Champagnes are made from organically or biodynamically farmed grapes. Why?

My belief is that a grower's practices tell you something about the grower and the producer (who may be the same). Anyone who cares about their Champagne vineyard so much that they have decided to avoid quick-fix chemicals, grow cover crops such as grass between vines, work the soil by hand, use only copper and sulfur in low amounts, treat parcels separately according to their needs, accept low yields in one year to promote a lifetime of vineyard health—all of which describe Emmanuel Lassaigne's practices—most likely gives a damn about making excellent Champagne. You wouldn't expect this level of commitment to end in the vineyard. It's no different in any other area of life: those who exercise great care, perhaps excessive care, in foundational or unnoticed details tend to produce superior results. To go to the trouble and take the risk of farming grapes in Champagne conscientiously, respectfully, and naturally is to demonstrate a love of the vines and the wine. This is the human element that converts the potential of vineyards like Le Cotet into magnificent Champagnes.

Not only is Montgueux not in the Côte des Blancs, it's in a different French administrative department, the Aube. In the world of Champagne, the Aube is best known as the home of yet another region underappreciated in the *échelle des crus* and beloved by experienced Champagne drinkers: the Côte des Bar.

Côte des Bar

To view Champagne as a collection of subregions is to see it as a theme park, a kind of adult Disneyland. On the one hand, the entire region is tied together by a regulated uniformity that is very unusual in the wine regions of France. Only one sparkling wine is made, and it must be produced in compliance with only one set of detailed rules. No matter where in the region the grapes are grown or the sparkling wines are produced, there is but one Champagne. Champagne's subregions are like the lands in a theme park. Fundamentally, you're getting the same product everywhere, but it's themed differently, enough so that each experience is distinctive. And if Champagne were Disneyland, then the Côte des Bar would be Frontierland. It's wild, fun, unpredictable, a mix of romanticism, enthusiasm, and rugged individualism. In the Côte des Bar, your glass of Champagne comes with a dose of adventure.

The source of the Côte des Bar's distinctiveness is its distance—almost a hundred miles—from the heartland of Champagne. The most obvious effect of the geographical separation is that the Côte des Bar generally is warmer than the subregions near the Marne. It is predominantly planted to Pinot Noir, which can ripen to such a degree that wines made from this variety in the Côte des Bar tend to be fruitier and softer than in the rest of Champagne. We saw a great example of this in Marie-Courtin Efflorescence, which is an abundantly fruity, round, and balanced *blanc de noirs* without dosage. But while natural, physical differences between the Côte des Bar and the Marne subregions are interesting and important, they are practically insignificant compared to the effects of a cultural rift that has existed for over a hundred years.

Power in Champagne is centered in the Marne department. There is very little power in the Côte des Bar. And that pretty well explains the last hundred years of the Côte des Bar getting the shaft. It was intentionally excluded from the first legal definition of the Champagne vineyard area in 1908, designated as a severely hampered "second zone" for Champagne in 1911, ignored in the 1911 *échelle des crus*, and, when eventually rated, given the lowest possible ratings (all 64 Côte des Bar villages ended up at the minimum 80% in the final tally in 1985). To this day, the reputation of the Côte des Bar is adversely—and unfairly—affected by the historical dominance of Champagne interests in the Marne. This is not to say that one could not make reasonable distinctions or generalizations, or that the Côte des Bar has always produced superior Champagne grapes. For example, before World War II, a significant amount of Gamay was planted here. But it's worth observing the tendency to view wine classifications as if somehow they derived wholly from nature and reason, when in truth they are created by human beings and are born of interests. Once you can see that clearly, it's much easier to appreciate that there are villages, growers, producers, and Champagnes in the Côte des Bar that are in no sense inferior.

But whatever the merits of the Côte des Bar's treatment as a second-class citizen, the effects are fairly clear. The Côte des Bar is, to some extent, a young wine region, with estate bottled Champagne mostly a phenomenon of the last fifty years. What you sense from grower-producers here is that they aren't particularly concerned with many of Champagne's traditions and dogmas. Why would they be, when part of the canon has been that the Côte des Bar is unworthy? This is why you will hear growers in the Côtes des Bar say they feel more of a spiritual connection with Burgundy. Burgundy isn't clamoring to take them in, but at least it never kicked them out. What you see in the Côte des Bar is the daring spirit of curious, enthusiastic people who are not burdened by the weight of expectations. This is where growers produce Champagnes made from one or more of Champagne's scorned grapes—Arbane, Petit Meslier, Pinot Blanc, and Pinot Gris—and evidently are proud to do so. It's where, as we saw in Chapter 2, Bertrand Gautherot of Vouette & Sorbée produces a fascinating, numinous *blanc de blancs* of Chardonnay in a place known for plump Pinot Noir. And it's where convention-challenging choices surrounding viticulture, sulfur, atmospheric pressure, dosage, aging, and the like are just part of the expected landscape. The Côtes des Bar has become a laboratory constantly producing new, interesting Champagnes that, collectively, are a feast for the inquisitive Champagne drinker.

Just as a Disneyland guest needs Frontierland, a Champagne drinker needs the Côte des Bar. It adds to the overall experience, the adventure. And that brings us to our final two wines.

Drappier Grand Sendrée

One of the oldest, most storied houses of the Côte des Bar also perfectly represents the character of today's growers and producers in this corner of Champagne. The Drappier family has been tending vines in the Côte des Bar for over two hundred years and was a motivating force behind the conversion of the area's vineyards to Pinot Noir in the 20th century. Today, Drappier's outstanding Champagnes reflect the results of dedication, experimentation, and innovation.

Drappier is a prime example of a house that pays great attention to details in a way that suggests the exercise of care at a higher level than necessary. It farms organically, as many other responsible growers do, but it also has extended its environmentally sound practices to its entire operation, becoming the first Champagne house to be certified as carbon neutral. In the cellar, Drappier goes to the expense of riddling and disgorging small- and large-format bottles of all sizes, including thirty-liter monsters, even though the law does not require it and few consumers would ever notice. In the last stage of Champagne production, Drappier probably invests more in its *liqueur d'expédition* than any other Champagne house. The choice of what wine to use to top up bottles after disgorgement varies in Champagne, but Drappier utilizes wines that it first matures in casks and then stores for over a decade, in an effort to contribute concentration and complexity in the bottle with what amounts to a tiny percentage of the total volume of wine. Does Drappier care deeply about the quality of its Champagnes? You tell me.

Of course, I hope we all will be drinking high-quality, distinctive, interesting Champagnes not just today, but for many years to come. And for that to happen, we need producers whose efforts go beyond mere sustainability, to creativity and growth. For example, Drappier is one of a handful of producers who are experimenting with aging Champagnes underwater in an attempt to slow down the aging process. Drappier actually started by aging Champagnes in the Alps but determined that the wines aged too quickly. Then Drappier went in the other direction and submerged its wines thirty meters in a bay off the coast of Brittany. Nobody knows for sure where this might take Champagne in the long term, and the same can be said for Drappier's reduced use of sulfur in the winemaking process. Amounts of sulfur are not high in Champagne, and sulfur is considered necessary to prevent premature oxidation. But Drappier believes that lowering sulfur levels is beneficial not just from the perspective of human health and sensitivity, but that it also improves the aromatics and texture of Champagne. It has developed one Champagne with no sulfur or dosage, and the rest of its line sees very low levels of sulfur. At the very least, Drappier's work in this area is demonstrating what is possible today, and it could lead to an evolution in the Champagnes of tomorrow.

This brings me to Drappier's top cuvée, Grand Sendrée, which expresses beautifully the past, present, and possible future of the Côte des Bar. Grand Sendrée is made from a few plots of Pinot Noir and Chardonnay in Urville, Drappier's home village since its founding in 1808. It's a single-vineyard Champagne, one of the early members of this category when it was first released from the 1975 vintage. Today, about a third of the wine is aged in oak, and it receives a fairly low level of dosage and very little sulfur. Grand Sendrée is similar to every other great Champagne, in that it is like a person who is not only well dressed but who also is undeniably yet somehow ineffably "put together." I have referred to a few Champagnes in this book as being rich, and Grand Sendrée is classically rich Champagne. In Grand Sendrée, richness is found in a blend of elements: ripeness and warmth of fruit, not high-toned citrus but concentrated apricots and nectarines; mellow autolytic notes, not of toast but of steaming biscuits; a mouthfeel that is more coating than zesty; and a slight undercurrent of oxidative flavors. All of these elements work together, and none is out of place or absent at any phase of drinking Grand Sendrée. But rich Champagne cannot be great if it is overbearing and not mouthwatering. What makes Grand Sendrée great Champagne, what makes it "put together," is that complex and delicious richness is moderated and harmonized by the lightness and freshness we expect from Champagne. The wine invites you into peak experiences of flavor and texture, but it doesn't hold up and weigh you down. It moves on and leaves your mouth watering in its wake. That, in essence, is what Champagne does at its best. It delights, intrigues, and refreshes.

There will always be those wine drinkers who feel compelled to hold on to old divisions, grades, and hierarchies, as if "knowing" that the Côte des Bar is a lesser subregion is a comfort rather than a self-imposed limitation. For the rest of us, for the Champagne explorers in search of joy wherever it may be found, there is possibility, and there is Drappier Grand Sendrée.

OLIVIER HORIOT ROSÉ DES RICEYS EN BARMONT

When Olivier Horiot began making wine in 2000 in Les Riceys, at the southern edge of Champagne, he did not make Champagne. Instead, he started producing still wines that have been made for a much longer period of time in the Champagne region. He made one of these wines—Rosé des Riceys—in two different single-vineyard bottlings, with such results that he soon became a standard bearer for this wine, which almost had fallen into complete obscurity. Along the way, he converted his vineyards to grow grapes organically and biodynamically, decided to make a range of single-vineyard, vintage, and blended Champagnes too, cultivated all seven Champagne varieties, greatly reduced the use of sulfur, and experimented with all manner of fermentation vessels and methods. In a nutshell, this is the Côte des Bar.

I hope by now you appreciate that in Champagne there usually is something new and interesting to be discovered around the corner, if only you look. And in the spirit of adventure, I thought I would end with a wine that is not Champagne but that is one of the jewels of Champagne. Rosé des Riceys is a still rosé unlike any other. It's what you might call an old-style rosé, and, in fact, it's been made for hundreds of years and purportedly was a favorite of King Louis XIV. Most modern rosés are made like white wines: grapes are pressed to obtain just enough color from the skins to make the wines pink; they are fermented at cool temperatures in stainless-steel tanks to preserve light aromatics; and they are bottled without aging and released immediately. Rosé des Riceys is made the opposite way—like a red wine from Pinot Noir (the only approved grape variety) that is just slightly less extracted.

Olivier Horiot makes a much bigger commitment to this unique wine than he needs to. En Barmont is a single-vineyard rosé that is made by semi-carbonic maceration, in which a portion of the grapes are crushed, and the rest are included in the fermentation vessel as whole bunches. The wines ferment slowly in small, used Burgundy barrels, where they remain for about a year. After Horiot finally bottles En Barmont and his other single-vineyard Rosé des Riceys (En Valingrain), he waits a few years before releasing them to the market. It's an expensive, time-consuming, and not particularly remunerative undertaking that is virtually unheard of for a still rosé.

The result is a wine that has much more color, character, and complexity than we have come to expect from rosés. En Barmont has a ruby color of moderate intensity, which you could mistake for a lightly colored red Burgundy. It's perfumed and very fruity, with complements of herbs and spices and a tinge of confection. The texture is soft and gentle, quite unlike so many tart rosés that lack enough fruit to balance their biting acidity. There is yet another fundamental character to the wine that is somewhat hard to describe—a savory, oxidative, nutty underpinning that is part of the identity of Rosé des Riceys. The entire package might best be described, as it is locally, as "*goût des Riceys.*" The taste of Riceys—you just have to drink it to be in the know.

A reasonable person would not make Rosé des Riceys. There are so many more sensible things to do. Then again, a reasonable person wouldn't scour the Internet for bottles of a rare aged rosé when the supermarket down the street is fully stocked every day of the year with an assortment of perfectly acceptable, perfectly conventional, perfectly boring rosés. The way I look at it, though, intentionally rejecting reason in favor of obsession in one or two areas of life is itself reasonable. And if you're going to obsess about something, it's self-defeating to turn away from the obscure, the unpopular, the unconventional, and—most importantly—the absurd. Rosé des Riceys, like Champagne, is for the passionate. It's for the person who is excited to look around the corner in Champagne. Who knows what's around the next one?

Press the Button

THERE'S ANOTHER BUTTON MARKED "Press for Champagne," and it's hanging on a wall in the dining room of my home. Sure, it's only decorative and not hooked up to a kitchen. But it makes a ringing noise like an old-fashioned telephone when you press it, and it makes people smile and laugh when they see it. A few minutes ago, I did something I have done many, many times before: I pressed the button.

You probably won't be surprised to hear that when I press this button Champagne is poured. Sure enough, not long after hearing the ring of the bell, I delivered to myself a glass of Pierre Péters Cuvée de Réserve. Using this book as a guide, you could piece together a picture of the Champagne I'm drinking right now. It's a *blanc de blancs* made entirely of Chardonnay grown in Grand Cru villages of the Côte des Blancs, and it's a bright, refreshing Champagne with subtle lemon and toasty notes. It's made reductively, showing no oxidative aromas and presenting as light on the palate. At the same time, there is a certain depth and richness to this Champagne, as it's a non-vintage Champagne that contains old reserve wines. The dosage of six grams per liter does not make the Champagne sweet but is consistent with the overall style of the wine. The back label says the Champagne was disgorged more than four years ago, which is right in my personal zone of aging preference. I've learned to trust Pierre Péters to produce outstanding Champagnes at every price point, and at this very moment my trust is being rewarded. Though I've drunk this Champagne many times, I'm struck by how delicious it is and how happy I am to drink it right now. And if you were drinking this Champagne right now, perhaps that's the way you would feel too.

This book has guided you through Champagne in a way that is both objective and subjective—it's impossible for a drinker and the drinker's palate and personal preferences to be removed from the experience of tasting wine. And now that you have read this book, you are well on your way along the path of your individual, distinct journey into Champagne. You understand the effects of choices made in Champagne. You know how Champagnes can differ based on which grape varieties are used and how and where they are grown, how the vast array of winemaking choices can lead to a multiplicity of different wines, and how even the mindset and attitudes of a grower or producer can affect what you experience in a bottle of Champagne. You've also seen the myths and misstatements in Champagne, and you understand how to process them. The primary benefit of this knowledge is not the ability to correctly identify and describe a Champagne. It's that you now have the tools to explore Champagne for yourself and the ability to unlock what Champagne has to offer, to you. Your Champagne drinking experiences and preferences likely will vary from mine. If you use what you've learned in this book to explore Champagne, and you decide that any of my opinions are completely wrong, I'll be happy for you because you will know Champagne for yourself.

The true key to enjoying Champagne is to be curious and to act on your curiosity. Put down this book and drink Champagne! Drink it as soon as the opportunity presents; drink it as often as is feasible under the circumstances; drink it alone when you feel like it and with others when they want to join in; drink it with enthusiasm and inquisitiveness. And drink it joyfully. Press the button.

Map of Champagne

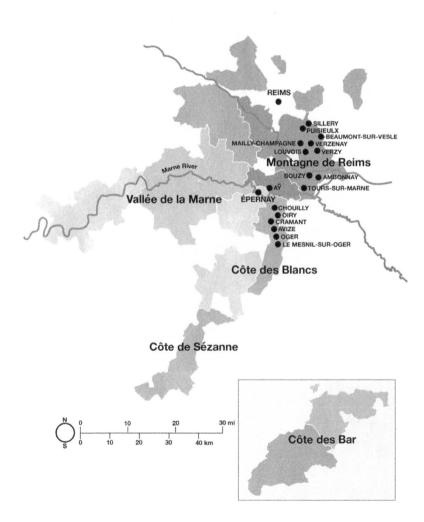

REIMS

SILLERY
PUISIEULX
BEAUMONT-SUR-VESLE
MAILLY-CHAMPAGNE • • VERZENAY
LOUVOIS • • VERZY

Montagne de Reims

Marne River

BOUZY • • AMBONNAY
AŸ • • TOURS-SUR-MARNE
ÉPERNAY

Vallée de la Marne

CHOUILLY
OIRY
CRAMANT
AVIZE
OGER
LE MESNIL-SUR-OGER

Côte des Blancs

Côte de Sézanne

N
0   10   20   30 mi
S   0   10   20   30   40 km

Côte des Bar

Made in the USA
Las Vegas, NV
01 November 2022

58587752R00111